Jocelyn Green and [illegible] other writers in this book have connected to the hearts of military wives with compassion, grace, and hearts full of mercy. These writers have been there and have brought to us as readers compelling devotions to connect us to the Lord, our spouse, and the hope of a strong marriage during times of deployment. In all the work we have done in reaching out to military marriages, this resource is the best tool we have found for ministering to the spiritual needs of these heroic couples serving our great nation.

DR. GARY AND BARB ROSBERG, *America's Family Coaches Authors,* 6 Secrets to a Lasting Love, *national radio show cohosts, and founders of The Great Marriage Experience*

The messages of the *Faith Deployed* devotionals resonated with me greatly, on so many levels. As testified to by the contributing authors, we are all challenged with trusting in God's plan, being married to the military, and loving our community in spite of fear, doubt, and depleted emotional reserves. But only by doing the first, trusting God, can we do the rest (over and over again). This book reminds us—through wonderfully appropriate Bible passages—of specifically that point. It doesn't dismiss our hard times but gives us hope and instruction on how to break through. I'm excited for all those who needed such a book as this—who knows what new heights it can bring our relationships with God, our husbands, and our communities?

STARLETT HENDERSON, Field Problems *co-author and Army Wife Talk Radio co-host*

This book will uplift you and give you the courage to press on, the comfort that you are not alone, and a hope that is grounded in the promises of God. A must read!

REV. RAHNELLA ADSIT, *Military Ministry, Campus Crusade for Christ International and coauthor of* When War Comes Home: Christ-centered Healing for Wives of Combat Veterans

Good morale is essential to good military functioning, and an essential element to military morale is what's happening on the home front. Jocelyn Green writes to those thousands of military wives left to tend the home fires as their husbands deploy around the world—often for more than a year at a time. Grounded in solid, practical, been-there advice and rooted in biblical truth, *Faith Deployed* should be essential reading for everyone whose husband serves in uniform.

TOM NEVEN, *Focus on the Family Editorial Director, Marine Corps veteran, and author of* On the Frontline: A Personal Guidebook for the Physical, Emotional, and Spiritual Challenges of Military Life

Faith Deployed is one of those rare books that totally delivers what it promises—daily encouragement for those brave, unsung heroes who are called to be *military wives.* I offer my highest commendation to Jocelyn Green and the other outstanding contributors to this book, who have done a masterful job of crafting this inspiring collection of practical wisdom. The life of a military wife is filled with persistent stresses, unending demands, and unique challenges that at times can seem overwhelming. This wonderful resource will powerfully connect with and impact the hearts of all those who courageously face these daily battles. I heartily recommend this book to you—the Christ-honoring, biblically rooted, and faith-strengthening words of encouragement you will find could change your life forever!

RON HOLECHEK, *director, The Navigators Military Ministry; vice president, The U.S. Navigators*

Certainly military wives need help and hope for their critical role in maintaining strong families, supporting their military man, and serving our nation's future. In *Faith Deployed,* Jocelyn Green has focused the relevance of God's Word on the realities of life as a military wife. I strongly recommend these doses of encouragement as a powerful antidote to the compassion fatigue so prevalent in today's military families. May the readers truly "March on with strength, O my Lord" (Judges 5:21).

BOB DEES, *Major General, U.S. Army, Retired; Executive Director, CCCI Military Ministry, www.militaryministry.org*

Military wives daily face unique and multifaceted stresses as they seek to love their husbands and children in the midst of the ever-challenging, as well as the ever-rewarding, life they experience in the military community. These brave women deserve our nation's gratitude and honor. They also deserve Jocelyn Green's wonderful book *Faith Deployed*, which richly and powerfully connects biblical principles to the varied rigors and blessings of their daily lives. A must-read not only for our military wives, but also for those who would seek to know, understand, and love them better.

DAVID SCHROEDER, *President, Cadence International*

Fresh and engaging! My salute to Jocelyn Green, who has put together a rich anthology of the choicest tidbits of spiritual nurture for military wives. It is carefully crafted to lift the spirit and soul of those who have struggled to see God's grace embedded in their oft-jumbled lives of deployed husbands and short-notice moves; of expectations to be both mother and father to the children of America's warriors; and of the unique demands that military life somehow places on them. A true companion to the Bible for military wives.

CHAPLAIN (COLONEL) CHIP FOWLER, *U.S. Army, Retired*

DEPLOYED

Daily Encouragement for

★ Military Wives ★

JOCELYN GREEN

MOODY PUBLISHERS

CHICAGO

Editor: Pam Pugh
Cover design: Dog Eared Design
Cover image: iStockphoto.com
Interior design: Smartt Guys design

Library of Congress Cataloging-in-Publication Data

Green, Jocelyn.
Faith deployed : daily encouragement for military wives / by Jocelyn Green.
p. cm.
Includes bibliographical references.
ISBN 978-0-8024-5250-4
1. Wives--Prayers and devotions. 2. Military spouses--Religious life. 3. Devotional calendars. I. Title.
BV4528.15.G73 2009
242'.6435--dc22
2008020885

Published in association with the literary agency of Sanford Communications, Inc., Portland, Oregon, www.sanfordci.com.

We hope you enjoy this book from Moody Publishers. Our goal is to provide high-quality, thought-provoking books and products that connect truth to your real needs and challenges. For more information on other books and products written and produced from a biblical perspective, go to www.moodypublishers.com or write to:
Moody Publishers
820 N. LaSalle Boulevard
Chicago, IL 60610

5 7 9 10 8 6 4

Printed in the United States of America

Dedication

In memory of Navy wife and author Denise McColl,
who was devoted to her husband and daughters
and to nurturing other military wives until cancer
took her life in March 2008.

Dedicated to the wives of all those who serve our country
through the U.S. armed forces, especially Army spouses
who often endure repeated lengthy deployments.

Section Three

Ambassadors for Christ: Viewing Our Role as a Ministry

Section Four

Taking Orders: Living the Life That Has Been Set before Us

Section Five

Total Surrender: Giving Up Our Attempts to Be in Control

Section Eight

Hope of Victory: Recognizing God's Goodness

Acknowledgments

I wish to express my heartfelt gratitude to my agent, David Sanford, for being the first one to believe in this book and champion the project, along with Rebekah Clark, Elizabeth Jones, Alyssa Hoekman, and the dedicated SCI team. Thanks to the talented team at Moody Publishers for bringing this book to fruition.

I'm so grateful for my fellow writers in this book, who I admire so much for their strength and wisdom: Pamela Anderson, Sarah Ball, Rebekah Benimoff, Paulette Harris, Jill Hart, Sara Horn, Denise McColl, Lori Mumford, Vanessa Peters, Lasana Ritchie, Sheryl Shearer, Ronda Sturgill, Marshéle Carter Waddell, and Eathel Weimer. Without the contributions of these women, this book would not be possible.

Thanks also to the women who have shared their stories of military life with me as I prepared this book: Rachel Bjorn, Ann Hardin, Melissa Gardner, Leisa Gustafson, Deshua Joyce, Ellie Kay, Amy MacLeod, Jill McMillan, Patti Morse, Brandy Shutt, and Mary Whitlock.

Finally, thanks to my husband, Rob, for his continual support of this work.

Introduction

If you have ever felt overlooked and undernourished as you strive daily to meet the needs of everyone around you—in a culture that largely does not understand your stressful lifestyle—this book is for you. *Faith Deployed* is not a guide to long-distance relationships or a how-to on navigating through the military culture. It does not offer "ten easy steps" for an easier, painless life. Instead, through squarely addressing the challenges you face, *Faith Deployed* will equip you to respond biblically to the daily struggles that threaten to wear you down.

How does the Christian military wife maintain a strong sense of patriotism without allowing her country to become an idol? What good can possibly come from moving every two to three years? How can I be sure that God has a purpose for my life that is just as strong as His purpose for my husband's?

With contributions from fifteen Christian wives from each branch of the armed services, *Faith Deployed* explores all these questions and more. The foundation of this book is the unchanging character of God. Our hope is not tied to shifting circumstances, but is anchored in the person of Jesus Christ. I pray that you know Him personally already. If you don't, or if you're unsure, please see the appendix on this subject in the back of the book.

As you read about how the Bible relates to what you are experiencing in the military community, my prayer is that your faith will be strengthened, your heart will be encouraged, your eyes will be turned toward Jesus, and that each of you will be able to echo the last stanza of the classic hymn "Be Thou My Vision":

High King of heaven, when victory is won,
May I reach heaven's joys, O bright heaven's Sun!
Heart of my own heart, whatever befall,
Still be my Vision, O Ruler of all.[1]

Section One

TAKING EVERY THOUGHT CAPTIVE:

Training Our Minds to a Biblical Perspective

For though we walk in the flesh, we do not war according to the flesh, for the weapons of our warfare are not of the flesh, but divinely powerful for the destruction of fortresses. We are destroying speculations and every lofty thing raised up against the knowledge of God, and we are taking every thought captive to the obedience of Christ.

2 CORINTHIANS 10:3–5

by Jocelyn Green

THE *Gift* OF SOLITUDE

Be still and know that I am God.
PSALM 46:10

★ ★ ★

IT WAS A FAMILIAR RITUAL OF MINE: after dropping my husband off at his ship for a month-long patrol, I drove home with the radio on and steeled myself for the empty house awaiting me. Since we were in Alaska, it was usually still dark at this time of day and would be for several more hours, which only seemed to sharpen my sense of loneliness. When I arrived home, I'd flip on all the lights and turn on the TV to fill the void of silence that always came when Rob was at sea.

I was newly married, with no children yet, and living off base. I kept myself as active as I could. If I was particularly lonely, I called another Coast Guard wife. While quiet solitude offered itself to me every day, it was the absolute last thing I wanted (remember this is *before* I had children!).

And yet, by casting solitude aside, I also shrugged off the opportunity to reflect, to fellowship with God and hear His voice, to just be still and know that He is God. Solitude means withdrawing from conversation, from the presence of others, from noise, from the constant barrage of stimulation. It is something that Jesus himself sought after while he was on this earth. The gospel of Luke says that "Jesus often withdrew to lonely places and prayed" (Luke 5:16 NIV). If Jesus, who was perfect and divine, needed to seek out solitude to be renewed and restored, and to receive grace and direction from the Father, how much more do we as mere mortals need to do the same?

Jill McMillan, whose Marine husband was often deployed, thrives in the company of others. She says, "And yet, the Lord told me, 'You don't need to be always in on the action. Go to the lonely places like Christ did.' That's when I really grow close to the Lord."

One writer says this: "Strength is in quietness. The lake must be calm if the heavens are to be reflected on its surface. Our Lord loved the people, but how often we read of His going away from them for a brief season. . . . The one thing needed above all others today is that we shall go apart with our Lord, and sit at His feet in the sacred privacy of His blessed presence. Oh, for the lost art of meditation! Oh, for the culture of the secret place! Oh, for the tonic of waiting upon God!"[1]

While I was trying so hard to withdraw from what I thought were the lonely places, I should have taken my cue from Jesus and let myself enter into those places of quiet to pray. To dwell on the fact that no matter what I was going through, God is still God, and miraculously, He wants to spend time with me.

Ask

Am I jam-packing my life so much that I have no time to pause before the Father? What is keeping me from sharing moments of stillness with God?

Pray

Lord, You see how hard I fight against loneliness. You know I am trying to stay engaged in my community so that I don't have time to notice the pangs of emptiness that seek to assault me. But in my efforts to crowd out those aching feelings, let me not neglect my time alone with You. I need to be recharged by Your Spirit. Comfort me with Your presence today. In Jesus' Name, Amen.

by Jill Hart

Blessed CONTENTMENT

I have learned to be content
whatever the circumstances.
PHILIPPIANS 4:11 NIV

★ ★ ★

DURING OUR FIRST YEARS of marriage we, like many military families, lived frugally. I worked full-time at a job I dreaded each morning, but dreamt of starting a family and staying home to care for them. As time went on, it became my focus and each day began to revolve around my desire to be a stay-at-home mom.

While the goal was admirable, my attitude was not. I began to resent having to work, which caused stress on my marriage. Fed up with my constant grumbling, my husband made a comment that changed my life. He said, "Jill, why don't you stop complaining, trust God to see you through, and start looking for a way to work from home?"

His statement made me reevaluate my attitude, and it ultimately launched what would become my own home-based business. However, what he said to me that day did even more than that. It made me realize that instead of being thankful for all God had given me and looking forward to what He may have in store, I had been focusing solely on the negative aspects of my life.

How could I possibly have a good attitude or find success when the only things I could see were the things I was unhappy with? That day, I sat down and made a list of things both big and small that I am grateful for. I keep the list in the top drawer of my desk and anytime I find myself with an attitude of discontent or grumbling, I pull out that list and read through it. It's such a powerful reminder to be thankful no matter what my situation in life. Even in times where we have found ourselves with more bills than money, He has been faithful and seen us through.

A great example of contentment in the face of trials is Horatio Spafford. Spafford lost much during his life—real estate that provided his living burned in the Chicago Fire of 1871, a son died about that same time, and four daughters were lost when their ship sank crossing the Atlantic. In the midst of these tragedies, Spafford met with his good friend, evangelist D.L. Moody. He reportedly told Moody, "It is well. The will of God be done." It was these words that eventually led him to pen the well-known hymn "It Is Well with My Soul."

During his time as a missionary, the apostle Paul was loved by some, beaten and imprisoned by others, and yet always content. Philippians 4:11b–13 (NIV) gives us a glimpse of his attitude: "...I have learned to be content whatever the circumstances. I know what it is to be in need, and I know what it is to have plenty. I have learned the secret of being content in any and every situation, whether well fed or hungry, whether living in plenty or in want. I can do everything through him who gives me strength."

Ask

What is my attitude?
Am I grateful for all I've been given or focused on what I don't have?
How can I develop an attitude that pleases God?

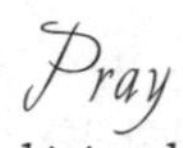

Dear Lord, You know how hard it is to be grateful when circumstances are difficult. Help me to keep my eyes on You, knowing that You have what's best for me at heart. Help me to be content no matter what my situation. In Jesus' Name, Amen.

by Sarah Ball

In Everything Give Thanks

In everything give thanks; for this is
God's will for you in Christ Jesus.
1 Thessalonians 5:18

★ ★ ★

GIVE THANKS in all circumstances? I think I'd be much more comfortable with this verse if it said: "Give thanks to God in as many circumstances as possible, excluding car breakdowns, child behavior problems, and deployments." After all, who could possibly expect me to be thankful during deployments?

The uncomfortable answer to that question: God does. God expects and desires my thanksgiving in all circumstances. God does not command us to be thankful *for* everything, but we are expected to give thanks *in* everything. I was relieved to realize that I didn't have to be thankful for deployments, but convicted of my need to continue praising God even during deployments.

Picture the scene of Shadrach, Meshach, and Abed-nego with me. Three young Jewish men, taken from their homeland to serve in a foreign land, are going head to head with the king of an empire. King Nebuchadnezzar orders them to bow and worship his statue, and they refuse. He threatens them with death in a fiery furnace, and this is their reply:

"Shadrach, Meshach, and Abed-nego replied to the king,

'O Nebuchadnezzar, we do not need to give you an answer concerning this matter. If it be so, our God whom we serve is able to deliver us from the furnace of blazing fire, and He will deliver us out of your hand, O king. But *even if He does not*, let it be known to you, O king, that we are not going to serve your gods or worship the golden image that you have set up'" (Daniel 3:16–18, emphasis added).

Shadrach, Meshach, and Abed-nego did not know how God would act in their circumstances. In their lives, they had seen times when God provided safety and times when God allowed His people to suffer. They did not know if God would intervene, but they trusted Him completely, and they were prepared to praise Him all the way to the furnace.

The challenge is to recognize that God could choose to shower us with blessings—but regardless of whether He chooses to do so, we are to give thanks. God could keep my husband here at home with me all the time, but if not, I will thank God for the husband He has given me. God could give my children hearts of perfect obedience every day, but if not, I will thank God for being their Heavenly Father, who holds my children in His own hands. God could PCS (permanent change of station) my family to a warm and sunny climate near the beach where housing is abundant and the cost of living is low, but if not, I will thank God that He never leaves me alone, no matter where I am.

Ask

Do I give thanks in all circumstances,
even those that are challenging or difficult?
Does my attitude of praise give glory to God
in front of other people?

Dear Lord, I thank You for Your Word, which challenges and encourages me. I thank You for sending Your Son to provide my salvation, so that I can live in hope, regardless of my circumstances. I thank You also for _________ (fill in your own list here, as long as you like!). Give me a heart of gratitude so that I may praise You in every situation. In Jesus' Name, Amen.

by Jocelyn Green

COMPARING *Trials*

Bear one another's burdens,
and thereby fulfill the law of Christ.
GALATIANS 6:2

★ ★ ★

I SAT IN OUR BIBLE STUDY and watched another woman share a prayer request. She was having a hard time dealing with the fact that her parents and sister's family had moved across the country. After years of living in the same small town of Homer, Alaska, this woman missed them terribly and was growing bitter about it.

As I listened to her share with broken voice and many tears, I'm ashamed to admit I had no compassion for her whatsoever. The first thing that jumped into my mind was, "You call that bad? Try being a military wife! We hardly ever get to live near our extended families. We don't even live with our own husbands half the time!"

I carried my "I have it worse than you" attitude home with me that day. I snuggled up to it to make myself feel more virtuous or worthy somehow. But the tighter I held on to it, the less Christ was able to use me. I used my own trials as something to be proud of. What a ridiculous thing to boast about!

Proverbs 14:10 says, "The heart knows its own bitterness, and a stranger does not share its joy." When I read that verse, it seems to tell me that each person's burden causes him or her a pain that should not be diminished just because someone else has it worse. It is impossible and worthless to compare trials. A truly humble person would have compassion and bear others' burdens no matter how they "rank" next to my own.

John Ortberg says this: "Humility . . . involves a healthy self-forgetfulness. We will know we have begun to make progress in humility when we find that we get so enabled by the Holy Spirit to live in the moment that we cease to be preoccupied with ourselves, one way or the other."[2] When we are with others, we're not assigning value to their prayer requests and feeling more spiritual if our own trials seem more acute.

In Galatians 6:2, Paul does not say, "Bear one another's burdens only if you deem the burden of sufficient magnitude. If it isn't a big deal to you, go ahead and let your sister in Christ figure it out on her own. She'll get over it." We are to "bear one another's burdens"—period.

Philippians 2:4–5 tells us, "Do not merely look out for your own personal interests, but also for the interests of others. Have this attitude in yourselves which was also in Christ Jesus." Now, if anyone had the right to consider other people's complaints as petty, Jesus did. Jesus knew He would die a horrific death on the cross to pay for the sins of the people who put Him there—and yet He took time to comfort and heal thousands of people with lesser trials. May we seek to model Jesus' humility and compassion in our own lives.

Ask

Am I harboring feelings of being more spiritual because of the difficult circumstances the military has given me?

How can I communicate love and understanding for other people this week?

Lord, It's so easy to focus on my own troubles. Please grant me the humility to set them aside so I can be genuinely available to minister to my brothers and sisters in Christ without comparing our burdens. Help me get my mind off myself by serving other people this week. In Jesus' Name, Amen.

by Marshéle Carter Waddell

Rank

Man looks at the outward appearance,
but the Lord looks at the heart.
1 SAMUEL 16:7

★ ★ ★

ONE MORNING, as my husband dressed for the day, I sensed his anxiety. He was to be the ringmaster of a dog and pony show for several captains and admirals scheduled to arrive that day. I put my arms around his neck, looked deep into his green eyes, and said, "Remember, Honey, the admiral puts his pants on one leg at a time, just like you." Mark relaxed.

There is danger in putting too much emphasis or value on a person's military rank. All personnel, from E-1 to O-10, share the same heart, mission, and vision for our nation. The only difference is in the duties assigned to each person. Rank and responsibilities differ; their souls, significance, and sacrifices don't.

The saying "You can't take it with you" is trite but right. Once an admiral, general, master chief, or sergeant major retires from military service, they can no longer command the same respect from the civilian world that they once did from the military realm. Sooner or later, the reality hits home that respect is earned, not assigned.

Our pastor has said that we should remember to take our "vitamin E" every day. He meant that a daily dose of looking at the eternal and getting our eyes off the things that pass away promotes health. God, His Word, and people are eternal. The black shoulder boards, gold stars, red stripes, colorful ribbons, and shiny medals will one day be placed and stored in a shadow box. Our bodies and worldly achievements, likewise, will be laid in a slightly larger box and given back to the dust. In the end, all that matters is our love for God and His highest creation, people. Friends and family are the only treasures that will survive beyond the grave. A daily dose of vitamin E-ternity can do much to correct an impaired view of people.

There is no partiality with God. Christ died for the private and the general alike. He came and died to redeem the seaman and the admiral, their wives and their children. Because He values and loves all of us equally, there should be no partiality in us. "Now then let the fear of the Lord be upon you; be very careful what you do, for the Lord our God will have no part in unrighteousness or partiality or the taking of a bribe" (2 Chronicles 19:7).

A chest full of ribbons and a shoulder heavy with stripes are not impressive to Him. "God sees not as man sees, for man looks at the outward appearance, but the Lord looks at the heart" (1 Samuel 16:7). Only humility, faith, and service move the heart of God.

Governments, rules, regulations, protocol, and etiquette are temporary. God wants us to live humbly in the present and to keep our focus on the eternal.

Ask

Do I assign value to people based on their rank?
How would the Lord rank my heart in comparison to His?

Lord, Thank You that You love us all the same. Thank you that You do not show partiality among Your children. Please give me eyes to see others the way You see them. Live Your life through me and cause me to love each individual regardless of where they currently rank in the world's value system. Enable me to give respect where it is due and keep my eyes focused on the eternal, priceless soul of each person who intersects my life today. In Jesus' Name, Amen.

by Sarah Ball

PRIVILEGED *Few*

How great is the love the Father has lavished on us,
that we should be called children of God!
And that is what we are!
1 JOHN 3:1A NIV

★ ★ ★

MY FIRST VISIT to the commissary was a landmark occasion. I wandered through the aisles with wide eyes, clutching my brand-new military ID, just in case someone questioned my right to be there. I was finally one of the few, the proud, the chosen—a military ID-holder with commissary and exchange privileges.

It seems silly to me now, but I spent years as a child longing to be allowed into the commissary and exchange. My missionary family lived overseas, and our only shopping options were little stores full of pricey, imported items. By contrast, our military friends shopped at their commissary and exchange, buying up-to-date items at fabulously low prices. My family would have loved to shop in the commissary or exchange, but the "Military ID-holders only" signs marked the stores as off-limits to us.

Today I came home from my usual commissary run and complained to my husband about the long wait at the checkout. The commissary is no longer a thrilling privilege; it's just another ordinary event in my week. I rarely stop to think about my military shopping privileges, unless I shop at a nonmilitary grocery store. The higher prices cause me to be thankful for the discounts I now take for granted.

In a small way, my military privileges remind me of my privileges as a child of God. When I accepted God's forgiveness of my sin and received the gift of salvation, I suddenly understood the words of the apostle John. It is amazing that God should love us, that He should accept us, that He should call us His children! What a privilege!

The privileges of being God's child are endless. I can pray to God as my heavenly father, knowing that He loves me and hears me. I can daily receive wisdom and patience to work with my children. I can rest each night in the unmatchable peace and comfort brought by the Holy Spirit. I can live my entire life with an eternal perspective, knowing that my life is not just about me, but about bringing glory to the God of the universe, with whom I will spend eternity.

I wish I could say that I respond to God's lavish love with my own abundant thanks and praise, but I'm afraid I fall short regularly. Everyday living has a way of making the divine become routine. The sense of awe I once felt spontaneously is now something I must actively seek.

In Psalm 105:4–5 NIV, David records one way that he maintained a thankful heart. "Look to the Lord and his strength; seek his face always. Remember the wonders he has done, his miracles, and the judgments he pronounced."

Did you see David's strategy? Relive the past. Remember what God has done for you. You and I have been granted incredible blessings as God's children. When we meditate on what we have received, we cannot help but praise God for calling us His privileged children.

Ask

How has my life changed since becoming a child of God?
Does my daily life reflect praise to God
for His lavish love and blessings?

Pray

Dear Father, Thank you for lavishing Your love on me and making me Your child. I recognize that my life is richly filled with many privileges and blessings. Help me to remember all You have done and to live in an attitude of ongoing thankfulness. In Jesus' Name, Amen.

by Jocelyn Green

BATTLE OF THE *Mind*

And do not be conformed to this world, but be transformed by the renewing of your mind, so that you may prove what the will of God is, that which is good and acceptable and perfect.
ROMANS 12:2

★ ★ ★

THE NUMBER OF VICTIMS killed in the terrorist attacks of September 11, 2001, is estimated at 2,973. At the time of this writing, there have been over four thousand American lives lost since the start of the Iraq war. These numbers don't even begin to tell the stories of soldiers who return home from Iraq or Afghanistan completely different people due to physical injury or post-traumatic stress disorder. In the face of such tragic realities, how are we to hold on to our faith in a loving, sovereign God?

According to Patti Morse, an Air Force wife of twenty-five years, "The battle for us begins and ends in the mind, and victory depends upon our consistent meditation on God's Word." Paul tells us in Ephesians 6:14 that the first piece of the armor of God we are to put on is Truth. Right thinking is to be our foundation.

Jerry Bridges says the three essential truths the Scriptures teach about God are that He is (1) completely sovereign; (2) infinite in wisdom; and (3) perfect in love. He writes: "Trusting God is not a matter of my feelings but of my will. That act of the will must be based on belief, and belief must be based on truth."[3]

When our hearts do not feel that God is still in control, we must consciously dwell on the truth of the Scriptures with our minds. Our thoughts can either drain our energy and cripple us, or be a source of strength when we meditate on God's Word.

David gives us a good look at his heart as he processes many trials. In many psalms, he does an absolute about-face between the first and last verses of the psalm. Psalm 13 begins with "How long, O Lord? Will you forget me forever?" By verse 5, he declares: "But I have trusted in Your lovingkindness; My heart shall rejoice in Your salvation. I will sing to the Lord, because He has dealt bountifully with me."

David seems to be doing something here that we can all learn from. While his heart may still be aching, he switches gears to focus not on what he feels, but on what he knows. And he knows who God is. He trusts in His character and remembers how the Lord has already taken care of him.

Proverbs 23:7 says, "For as he thinks within himself, so he is." The military wife who dwells in fear and anxiety for her husband's safety and her future will have little room in her heart for anything else. The one who dwells in God's Truth will be anchored, even through trials.

Ask

Am I allowing my feelings to take precedence
over what I know to be true of God?
How can I find more time in my day to read
and meditate on God's Word?

Pray

Lord, Help me to be like David—unafraid to cry out to You exactly how I'm feeling, but also able to turn my sorrow into reliance on Your truth by focusing on who You are. Break the bonds of fear, bitterness, and anything else that keeps me from resting in You, and teach me to be captivated by You alone. In Jesus' Name, Amen.

by Sheryl Shearer

THE STRUGGLE FOR *Contentment*

I have learned to be content whatever the circumstances. I know what it is to be in need, and I know what it is to have plenty. I have learned the secret of being content in any and every situation . . . I can do everything through him who gives me strength.

PHILIPPIANS 4:11–13 NIV

★ ★ ★

WHILE HANGING OUT with some officer wives from our Protestant Women of the Chapel (PWOC) group, one of the spouses blurted out excitedly that her husband was being promoted. Their family would be moving out of their apartment—the same housing that everyone else on the base inhabited except senior officers—into a house with a yard in which their small children could play. Instead of sharing her joy at the news, my heart sank.

Jealousy began to consume me shortly after we arrived in Germany for our first tour. Although he had prior military service, my husband reenlisted and had to begin anew as a private, an E-2. Both my husband and I had bachelor degrees, were pastors of a church, and were accustomed to being leaders. Being thrust into the military world of rank, status, privilege, and fraternization was a shock for me. I did not handle it well. I could not even drive through the officer housing area without my body tensing up from jealousy and resentment.

The resentment I harbored in my heart took some time to dissipate. Dissolving the hardness in my heart required serious soul-searching. Did my self-worth come from my possessions or my social status? I also had to acknowledge that insecurity and poor self-image were offshoots of jealousy.

Drawing strength from God through prayer, Scripture, and worship reminded me "to not be conformed to this world, but be transformed by the renewing of [my] mind" (Romans 12:2). Over time, I stopped comparing myself to others through the prism of rank and with a "worldly point of view" (2 Corinthians 5:16 NIV). Allowing Christ—not my circumstances—to define my self-worth set me on the road to freedom. I eventually began to see myself and others as Christ does.

One key ingredient to my heart change came as a result of the love extended to me by other Christian women. In our weekly PWOC group, I met and interacted with women of all ranks—including many whose husbands were senior officers—yet rank played no role in our relationships. These women befriended and accepted me because of me. They exemplified the attitude Jesus demands of His disciples: "Whoever wants to become great among you must be your servant, and whoever wants to be first must be slave of all" (Mark 10:43–44 NIV). God used their lives and gracious love to help me get past my prejudice, jealousy, and resentment.

A decade later, I am on the other side of the fence now that my husband is a Navy chaplain. Knowing how much I struggled with this issue, I am always sensitive to the matter. I remember the positive examples of those women and do my best to emulate them. Through Christ, I am able to love others with humility and equality—regardless of status or rank.

Ask

Am I jealous of others who have more than I do?
Do I look down on others who have lower rank?

Lord, Forgive me for any jealousy or resentment harboring in my heart. Help me to view others through Your eyes and not by their spouse's rank, status, or earthly possessions. Let me love and treat others as You would. In Jesus' Name, Amen.

by Jocelyn Green

CONQUERING *Resentment*

Do nothing from selfishness or empty conceit, but with humility of mind regard one another as more important than yourselves; do not merely look out for your own personal interests, but also for the interests of others.
PHILIPPIANS 2:3–4

★ ★ ★

SEVERAL COAST GUARD WIVES, including me, had crammed into an apartment living room for a book club meeting. As we chatted between bites of crackers and cheese, our conversation veered away from the book of the month when the hostess unleashed a bitter monologue concerning her husband's frequent absences at sea and punctuated it with a booming, "I did not sign up to be a single parent!" With one toddler and another baby due soon, this woman was clearly frazzled. Unfortunately, her resentment over having to be solo spilled out of her like a toxin and threatened to poison the evening.

Heroes at Home author Ellie Kay says resentment takes root when the focus is on our own unfulfilled desires and expectations, on why life isn't the way we want it to be right now. Our book club hostess, like most of us, desired for her husband to be a present father. Many wives struggle with not being able to pursue professional ambitions due to the transitory lifestyle of the military. And who doesn't wish we could spend more time with our families or friends we've left scattered all over the country?

Nancy Leigh DeMoss points out that no matter who we are (or what our husbands do for a living), we will always have unfilled longings this side of heaven (Romans 8:23). "It is important to understand that our inner longings are not necessarily sinful in and of themselves," she writes. "What is wrong is demanding that those longings be fulfilled here and now, or insisting on meeting those longings in illegitimate ways. . . . The second Truth is that the deepest longings of our hearts cannot be filled by any created person or thing. . . . We must learn to accept those longings, surrender them to God, and look to Him to meet the deepest needs of our hearts."[4]

Naomi and Ruth, both widowed and childless, certainly had unfulfilled longings when they returned to Bethlehem empty-handed. But instead of wallowing in their tragedy, Ruth rolled up her sleeves and went to work—hard work—gleaning in the fields under the hot sun so she could provide for herself and her mother-in-law.

When resentment threatens to infect our hearts, we need to take a cue from Ruth and step outside ourselves to serve others. "We are not going to change our husbands or the situation; we can't stop the war," says Ellie Kay. "If those things won't change, we must. The best way for a wife to stop resenting her husband's military service is for her to get out there and invest in the lives of other people. The number-one way is to start volunteering in her husband's unit. Or go out into the community and volunteer at homeless shelters, crisis pregnancy centers, your children's school. Once you start looking outside yourself to meet the needs of other people, a miracle happens. The very needs that had built resentment in your heart will turn around as you see God invited into the equation."

Ask

What resentment am I harboring that I should be giving to God?
How can I serve others this week?

Pray

Lord, Help me to surrender my unfulfilled desires to You, and to seek Your provision to meet the deepest needs of my heart. Show me how I might be used of You by looking to the interests of others (Philippians 2:4). In Jesus' Name, Amen.

by Sarah Ball

Heavenly THINGS

Since, then, you have been raised with Christ,
set your hearts on things above, where Christ is seated
at the right hand of God. Set your minds on
things above, not on earthly things.
COLOSSIANS 3:1–2 NIV

★ ★ ★

LAST YEAR, I teasingly told my children that I wanted a maid for Christmas. My four-year-old son looked confused for a minute. "But, Mom, we don't need a maid. You are the maid," he said.

Moments like that can make my life as an Army spouse and mother seem rather mundane. Most of my days are spent on "logistical support" for my family—laundry loads washed, grocery sacks purchased and hauled, doctor appointments kept, homework papers reviewed, and diapers changed. I often finish my day with our small military house messier than when I started. Can anyone relate?

I could easily lose sight of the purpose behind all the work. I need regular reminders that my everyday tasks are not about me, or even about my husband and children. I am part of the kingdom of God, so everything that I do should be about Him and His glory.

Colossians 3:1–2 challenge us to take our minds off the earthly things around us and set our hearts and minds on things above. Our new lives with Christ as children of God should have an eternal perspective. We have an incredible eternity in heaven ahead of us, and that should change everything about the way we see life on earth.

When I set my mind on things above, I realize that my job as a mother is primarily to teach my children to love and honor God. My words and actions need to clearly teach my children that their relationship with God is the only thing that will last for eternity.

When I set my mind on things above, I understand that my role as a wife is to honor my husband, giving him the respect and encouragement that he needs to fulfill God's purposes for him. Together, we are a God-ordained unit that can have an impact on soldiers and their families for Christ.

When I set my mind on things above, I see that my life is full of opportunities to do things with eternal importance. Every conversation, every action can be filled with the love of God and ultimately point people to Him.

I can be passionate about the assignments that God has given me right now—to be a soldier's wife and mother of four young children—because I see the eternal significance of these assignments. I can balance the tedium of endless housework and diaper changes by asking God, "What do You want me to do today? How can I use this day for Your purposes?" The work I do for God today may not be dramatic or glamorous, but it will last for all of eternity.

Ask

What assignments has God given me at this stage of my life?
Am I living each day with an eternal perspective,
seeking God's glory in my daily tasks?

Pray

Dear Lord, Thank You for giving my life a purpose and significance greater than myself and my circumstances. Please help me to set my mind on things above. Give me an eternal perspective, so I can see every part of my life as an opportunity to glorify You. In Jesus' Name, Amen.

Section Two

GUARDING THE HEART:

Protecting Ourselves from the World's Temptations

Watch over your heart with all diligence,
For from it flows the springs of life.

PROVERBS 4:23

by Jocelyn Green

AFFAIRS OF THE *Heart*

Watch over your heart with all diligence,
for from it flows the springs of life.
PROVERBS 4:23

★ ★ ★

A WOMAN in our Coast Guard unit had been corresponding with her old boyfriend for months, unbeknownst to her husband, e-mailing and instant messaging late into the night. She was convinced she would be happier if she filed for divorce, hoped for the best for her children, and returned to the arms of the one she did *not* marry.

While the geographical distance prevented her from having a physical relationship with this man, she was clearly in an emotional affair. Perhaps she thought that e-mailing couldn't hurt anything. But the more she shared of her heart with him, the more her desires bent toward being with him as a permanent solution to her loneliness and dissatisfaction in her own marriage.

The fact that it is common makes it no less tragic. Each one of us is vulnerable to the same situation. Those of us who would "never have an affair" might just be feeling lonely enough to mention it to a sympathetic man. If he offers us the male attention we are craving, if he makes us feel special, how can our hearts not want to go back for more? While not every emotional affair ends up in a physical affair, you can bet that every physical affair once began as an emotional affair.

Matthew 5:27–28 in *The Message* says, "You know the next commandment pretty well, too: 'Don't go to bed with another's spouse.' But don't think you've preserved your virtue simply by staying out of bed. Your heart can be corrupted by lust even quicker than your body. Those leering looks [or thoughts] you think nobody notices—they are also corrupt."

It's inevitable that you will notice attractive men—and that isn't sinful. It would be sinful if we allow that attraction to spur us on to develop an emotional attachment to that man. Here are some questions Shannon Ethridge suggests we ask ourselves to evaluate whether we, as married women, are in dangerous territory:

- Do you think of this man often (several times each day) even though he is not around?
- Do you select your daily attire based on whether you will see this person?
- Do you go out of your way to run into him, hoping he'll notice you?
- Do you wonder if he feels any attraction toward you?[1]

One way to play it safe and help guard our hearts is to guard our mouths. Flirting, complimenting, complaining, confessing, and inappropriate counseling and praying are all ways of communicating that could lead to a deeper relationship—in other words, avoid them!

If you find yourself struggling to reserve your heart's affections for your husband, seek out a trusted friend to serve as an accountability partner to you. You are less likely to stumble if you know you'll have to report it. "Iron sharpens iron, so one man sharpens another" (Proverbs 27:17).

Ask

Do I fantasize about what it would be like to be
with a different man?
When those thoughts cross my mind,
what can I do to starve those desires?

Pray

Lord, Help me guard my heart, especially when my husband is away. I know that Satan would love nothing more than to undermine my marriage and watch it fall apart. Alert me when my thoughts drift into inappropriate territory. Help me take every thought captive to Jesus Christ. In Jesus' Name, Amen.

by Lori Mumford

SURROGATE *Spouse*

You shall not commit adultery.
EXODUS 20:14

★ ★ ★

WE KNOW God forbids sexual relationships outside of marriage: that's adultery. Jesus told how adultery is a heart issue when you even lust after someone (Matthew 5:28). Most of us with often-absent husbands avoid close friendships with men outside of marriage because of possible temptations. But do most of us know to avoid a *kind* of adulterous friendship with a woman?

I believe adultery encompasses putting someone in the place that's reserved for your husband whether it be emotional, physical, sexual, mental, whatever. When areas are not met by our husband, and we don't ask God to fill these empty places with Himself, the Devil loves when we go looking elsewhere.

To make this clearer, I'm not talking about healthy friendships with women. That girlfriend who says, "Your husband just left. Would you like coffee together this morning?" That friend who brings dinner for you and says she's thinking and praying for you; or the one who offers to take your kids for a couple hours so you can be alone; that dear one who calls to encourage you with His Word: these are precious friendships. They don't fill the role of your husband. Rather, they graciously encourage you in your present circumstances.

I'm talking about the friend who **consistently** asks you to be in activities or places that you commonly share with your husband. It could be anything that you and your husband might enjoy together or just simply carry out together. Questions to ask yourself might be: would he mind if anyone else took his place in this? Or, does she ask much of your time even when your husband is home? Do you often prefer time with her over him? Does she say derogatory remarks about your husband? Do you often vent your frustrations with him to her?

The warning signs with adulterous women friendships are much harder to see coming, especially when you miss your husband; you're overwhelmed with responsibilities; and you're surrounded by women with needs like you. What better support than when someone empathizes with your challenges? Ask God to give you eyes to see when a woman wants an unhealthy friendship with you or when you may desire one yourself. It is our sinful nature that tries to fill voids with someone or something other than Him. Except for Him, nothing is fully satisfying: it's not meant to be. He wants to fill us with Himself and "supply all your needs according to His riches in glory in Christ Jesus" (Philippians 4:19).

So how do we handle a friendship like this? Love her, absolutely, but not necessarily the way she wants. Talk to her about reserved activities with your husband; excuse yourself from excessive phone calls or visits, especially when your husband is home; silence any words against him by declaring your love and thankfulness for him; direct her to the Lord if she tries to make you too important; and finally, pray for her and wisdom for yourself. If she no longer wants your friendship, let her go but keep praying for her.

Ask

Is a friend filling her husband's place with me?
Am I filling my husband's place or Your place
with someone else?

Lord, I don't want to take a husband's place nor Your place in anyone's life. Neither do I want to put anyone else in those places in my own life. Forgive me if I have done so unknowingly. Fill me so completely with You that I want nothing else. May others see You in me so that I can point them to You. In Jesus' Name, Amen.

by Vanessa Peters

FLEEING *Temptation*

Let us then approach the throne of grace with confidence so that we may receive mercy and find grace to help us in our time of need.
HEBREWS 4:16 NIV

★ ★ ★

I'VE BEEN TEMPTED by adultery exactly once in my seven years of marriage. It came on so suddenly and unexpectedly, I felt like I'd been blind-sided by the enemy. I am head over heels in love with my husband and have a beautiful marriage. Shame quickly rushed in as I asked myself, "How could I possibly be attracted to another man?"

Traveling without my husband, I stayed with some friends; also visiting in their home was an affectionate and attractive single man. I'm sure he meant no harm, but it was difficult for me to receive his attention in a nonromantic way. I found myself struggling inside, but embarrassed to admit my thoughts to anyone else.

The next morning, I opened my Bible for my daily devotion. I read in Proverbs 7 about a young man tempted by an adulteress who led him astray with persuasive words. The Proverb ends by saying that his affair cost him his life and warns readers to "not let [their] hearts turn to her ways or stray into her paths" (verse 25 NIV). The Bible was warning me about the very thing by which I was being tempted.

Next, I proceeded to Matthew 5, Jesus' Sermon on the

Mount. I came upon the following section: "I tell you that anyone who looks at a woman [or man] lustfully has already committed adultery ... in his [or her] heart" (v. 28 NIV). God really had my attention now!

I finished my devotion in the epistle of Hebrews. There I read, "We do not have a high priest who is unable to sympathize with our weaknesses, but we have One who has been tempted in every way, just as we are—yet was without sin. Let us then approach the throne of grace with confidence so that we may receive mercy and find grace to help us in our time of need" (Hebrews 4:15–16 NIV).

Oh, how I welcomed that invitation to boldly approach God's throne of grace. Jesus could relate to my wretched heart, and I was not alone in my struggle. I admitted my lustful thoughts, asked forgiveness, and prayed for help and strength to fight my sinful impulses. The freedom I experienced lifted my spirits, and I praised God for His perfect provision.

When I returned home, I confessed the thoughts I had entertained to my husband, who was graciously willing to forgive. As military wives, we're often faced with physical separation from our husband. While we don't usually think of ourselves likely to be tempted to stray, the Bible cautions us to be on guard. "So, if you think you are standing firm, be careful that you don't fall!" (1 Corinthians 10:12 NIV). We need to avoid potentially hazardous situations, surround ourselves with friends who will encourage us to be faithful, and be in the Word consistently—so that we keep our marriages pure and intimate, the way God desires.

Ask

Do I intentionally avoid tempting situations,
particularly when I'm not with my husband?
Do I have a proud heart that thinks adultery
could never happen to me?

Pray

Father, I want my marriage to be above reproach and bring glory to Your Name. Help me to honor my husband with my thoughts and actions, especially when we're apart. When I am tempted, give me "a way out so that [I] can stand up under it" (1 Corinthians 10:13 NIV). In Jesus' Name, Amen.

by Vanessa Peters

A *Marriage* WORTH FIGHTING FOR

So they are no longer two, but one flesh.
What therefore God has joined together, let no man separate.
MATTHEW 19:6

★ ★ ★

TONIGHT I LAY IN BED awake for a long time. I listened to my husband's sweet, rhythmic breathing as he slept beside me, and tried to imagine what life would be like without him there.

Earlier, I'd received news that some old friends of ours had divorced. This was a lovely family so similar to ours in many ways: my friend's husband attended the Air Force Academy along with mine, we were stationed at the same base, our husbands were in the same squadron and flew the same plane, we started having babies at the same time, and attended the same social functions. So, when the news came that this couple was now divorced and he was already remarried, leaving two scarred young children in the wake, my heart broke. I wept over a world gone wrong, Satan's victories at the very core of God's army—breaking apart the family.

The news was freshly poignant to me as David and I had recently experienced a significant fight in which tempers flared. In a moment of despair, I asked him, "Do you really think we'll make it?" Later, he prayed with me that I would see our marriage as worth fighting for. That really resonated with my heart.

What caused this beautiful family to break up? While I certainly don't know all the details, I consider this question quite soberly with the humbling realization that it could have just as easily been us. "So, if you think you are standing firm, ✗ be careful that you don't fall!" (1 Corinthians 10:12).

We know God desires marriages to be healthy and whole. "'I hate divorce,' says the Lord Almighty. . . . So guard yourself in your spirit, and do not break faith" (Malachi 2:16–17 NIV). But lest we think we are immune because we're Christians, let's consider the evidence: Over half of marriages in the United States end in divorce, and the rate among "Christian" marriages is no better. Some good friends of ours serve with Campus Crusade's Military Ministry. Their entire ministry is based on defending the military marriage. With staggering rates of troubled marriage and divorce in the military, exacerbated by deployment and war, they fight to keep these marriages together—for God's glory.

Relationships are hard, and in my own power, *my marriage* is surely on sandy ground. My own sinfulness will too often prevail when I rely on my strength. Yet, I have a powerful One who intercedes on my behalf when I am weak. He specializes in resurrecting that which would otherwise be dead. What assurance returned as I pondered the words of John Newton at age 82, soon to see Jesus face to face. The author of the famous hymn "Amazing Grace" was once a slave trader, then a sinner saved by grace, and later a powerful preacher: "My memory is nearly gone; but I remember two things: That I am a great sinner, and that Christ is a great Savior."[2]

Ask

Do I have a prideful attitude about marriage
and think that mine would never fail?
What am I doing to proactively protect my marriage now?

Lord Jesus, You created marriage for our good and Your glory. However, we live in a fallen world, and marriage is one of the most attacked institutions of our faith. Give us Your supernatural strength and grace to bind us together forever. Help me to be the kind of wife who fights fiercely for her marriage. In Jesus' Name, Amen.

by Jocelyn Green

PREEMPTIVE *Prayer*

Therefore, confess your sins to one another, and pray for one another so that you may be healed. The effective prayer of a righteous man can accomplish much.
JAMES 5:16

★ ★ ★

WHEN COUPLES ARE REUNITED after deployment, life doesn't exactly just fall right back into place. The post-separation stage is often a new beginning to marriage, requiring both husband and wife to learn how to be one again. And "becoming one" is especially challenging since the last several months have been spent quite independently.

To help overcome the instincts to look only to their own interests, many couples have found praying together to be mission-critical, a sort of preemptive measure with which to begin each day. When you begin the day by praying with your spouse, you are inviting God into your lives and are far more likely to react to challenges and miscommunications with God's perspective and grace.

James exhorts us to not just pray for one another, but to confess our sins to each other, too, as a part of the healing process (James 5:16). In my own life, I have often caught myself considering my husband's wrongs instead of my own. It's as if I am praying Psalm 139:23–24 back to God—but with all the wrong pronouns! "Search *him*, O God, and know *his* heart; Try *him* and know *his* anxious thoughts; And see if there be any hurtful way in *him*." If I really want God's power to be poured out on my marriage, I need to repent of my own anxious thoughts and hurtful ways and pray for the restoration that only God can give.

Jesus tells us, "Again I say to you, that if two of you agree on earth about anything that they may ask, it shall be done for them by My Father who is in heaven. For where two or three have gathered together in My name, I am there in their midst" (Matthew 18:19–20). You may think there is no way you can piece your marriage back together after the pressures of both separation and reentry. In our own power and strength, we can't. But when you and your husband agree to bring your marriage and each other's needs to the Lord in prayer, you are inviting the Almighty to be present with you, to fill you with grace, and to restore you back into the fullness of a godly marriage.

There is no burden so heavy that God cannot lift it from your shoulders, no valley so dark that He cannot shine His light and illuminate the path, no heart so broken that He cannot make it whole again. When you and your husband pray together, you grow closer to each other and to God.

Ask

What troubles could we be bringing to the Lord?
How can we fit a daily prayer time into our schedules?

Pray

Lord, Thank you for desiring the kind of relationship with Your children where we would come to You with our concerns. Help my husband and me to make daily prayer together a priority. When we are apart, help us find a way to pray on the phone or through e-mail so we stay connected to You as a couple. In Jesus' Name, Amen.

by Vanessa Peters

Married TO THE MILITARY

For this reason, a man will . . . be united to his wife, and they will become one flesh.
GENESIS 2:24 NIV

★ ★ ★

I WAS VISITING FRIENDS in Washington, D.C., trying not to miss my boyfriend, David, a student pilot in Mississippi. We were strolling around Georgetown University when suddenly I saw a handsome man in a suit walking confidently toward me. *David?!* I thought. It couldn't be! But there he was. He continued to walk toward me, and with a smile on his face, he kneeled on one knee and said, "Vanessa, I love you and can't imagine my life without you. I want to have a family with you. Will you marry me?" Only one thought screamed through my heart: "YES!" I'd never been more sure or happy in my life.

We'd recently spent late nights discussing the life of an Air Force wife. Having had no military experience, it was a whole new world for me. I heard stories from veteran Air Force wives of broken dishes and broken dreams. David communicated clearly that a marriage to him included a "marriage" to the military. He wanted my expectations to be realistic, and to be honest, I wasn't so sure I wanted that life.

But when it came down to it, God showed me that He would not call me to a life for which He would not equip me.

I loved David, and trusted that God's providence drew us together. If I loved everything about him, I loved the Air Force.

Years later, when I complained of long hours, deployments, and frequent moves, my husband would gently remind me, "It's an all-volunteer force, honey. We signed up." Our home-front role is just as vital as the military member's, and sometimes more difficult. As "one flesh," we tackle the job to serve and protect our nation together.

As women, we hold so much influence over our husbands' (and children's) attitudes. When my hubby knew I was safe and content, he could concentrate on completing his missions successfully. Our men are wired to be providers and protectors, so if they're worried about something at home or feel they're failing their families, their work suffers.

Proverbs 31 states: "A wife of noble character who can find? She is worth far more than rubies. Her husband has full confidence in her and lacks nothing of value. She brings him good, not harm, all the days of her life. . . . Her husband is respected at the city gate. . . . Her husband praises her" (verses 10–12, 23, 28 NIV). What a joy for a serviceman to have "full confidence" in his wife who "watches over the affairs of her household" (v. 27) while he cannot! We have a unique role to play in defending the country. While what we do may often seem like a "behind-the-scenes" and thankless job, our partners would be crippled without our support.

Even so, it's okay to ask for help. There have been times we've hired childcare or housecleaning services to ease the burden at home. Whatever the case, we must consider our role as encourager and supporter, and do it joyfully. "Give her the reward she has earned, and let her works bring her praise at the city gate" (Proverbs 31:31 NIV).

Does my husband have "full confidence" in me
when duty calls?
Do I have an attitude of commitment to the military
and joyfully serve alongside my soul mate?

Pray

Lord, You brought us to this place of self-sacrifice to protect our fellow man. I offer up the challenges to You and pray for courage when my own fails. Allow me to be a loving helper to my husband, who willingly defends our freedom. In Jesus' Name, Amen.

by Vanessa Peters

Idols of the Heart

Love the Lord your God with all your heart,
and with all your soul, and with all your mind.
MATTHEW 22:37

★ ★ ★

I HAVE A CONFESSION TO MAKE: I am a recovering Coke addict. Not the illegal white substance that lands you in rehab or jail; the Coke that in the South refers to all types of soda. My personal favorites are Dr. Pepper and Cherry Pepsi.

Although I've always enjoyed these drinks, only recently did I realize my addiction. It started when I was a single mom by default—my husband was TDY (Temporary Duty) or deployed, and I served as the sole caregiver for my young children. Some nights, I'd get little sleep and have to function the next day with no hope of Dad coming home that night. Coke became my crutch, or coping mechanism.

I'd arrange my schedule so I'd just "happen" to be driving by my favorite gas station with 50 cent-fountain drinks. I went from buying the 20-ounce to the 32-ounce—and on bad days, I'd resort to the 44-ounce. I'd make up excuses to buy two-liter bottles and end up consuming most of it myself.

Those of you reading this who have loved ones or themselves recovered from a devastating addiction to drugs or alcohol may have difficulty taking me seriously here. While the consequences of these addictions may be different, I contend that the root issues are quite similar.

C.S. Lewis said that our enjoyment of things lesser than the pleasures of God are like a child who chooses to make mud pies in a slum rather than enjoy a holiday at the sea: "We are half-hearted creatures, fooling about with drink and sex and ambition when infinite joy is offered us."[3] The military wife often faces trying circumstances that make her feel desperate to ease the pain, but we must learn to long for God alone. Only He can truly satisfy.

"Their idols are silver and gold, made by the hands of men. . . . Those who make them will be like them, and so will all who trust in them" (Psalm 115:4–8 NIV). The idols we think we can control end up consuming us. What seems a welcome escape actually ensnares and desensitizes us.

Each woman will struggle with her own idols. For some, it may be her own sweet husband, if in fact her desire for him surpasses her longing for God. For others, it may be food or children or an eating disorder that craves the perfect body. Certainly, many good things become idols. Augustine warned that too often we love gifts more than the Giver. For me, Coke became a consuming obsession and my own little idol.

We all struggle with them, and only an ultimate remedy will do. The power of the cross breaks the chains of addiction and bondage of idols in our hearts. When we release these competing loves and cling to our Savior, He brings deeper satisfaction that far outweighs them all.

Ask

What are the idols in my heart?
Am I willing to give up anything
that takes the place of God in my life?

Pray

Lord, I desire You alone. Free me from addictions that compete with my love for You, my greatest reward and highest pleasure. In Jesus' Name, Amen.

by Jocelyn Green

SILENT BUT *Guilty*

He who goes about as a slanderer reveals secrets,
Therefore do not associate with a gossip.
PROVERBS 20:19

★ ★ ★

ONE BLEAK WINTER DAY, I had lunch with other Coast Guard wives whose husbands were all at sea. By the end of my three hours with them, I had counted seven different women they had slandered on a variety of subjects, including fashion, weight, table manners, marital problems, child rearing, and spending habits. I remained uncomfortably silent through most of the conversations and was the first to leave, wondering what would be said about me when I was gone.

But what began as a spirit of righteous indignation on my part slowly gave way to a spirit of undeniable conviction. It is wrong to gossip, but it is just as wrong to listen to it. I wasn't off the hook just because I didn't speak much. My cowardly silence condoned what I heard; what's worse, I allowed the gossip to negatively influence my impressions of those who were the subjects of the conversations. That is sin! By remaining silent, I squandered an opportunity to be Christlike and steer the conversation in a more edifying direction.

Paul lists the sins of gossip and slander among the sins of murder and malice in Romans 1:28–32; they are to be taken very seriously. The problem is that gossip is so easy to do so often! As one of my friends told me, "We gossip whenever we get together because all we have in common is the other people in housing. So that's what we talk about."

Galatians 6:1 exhorts us to do more than just sit back and listen when we hear gossip or slander. "Brethren, even if anyone is caught in any trespass, you who are spiritual, restore such a one in a spirit of gentleness; each one looking to yourself, so that you too will not be tempted." In other words, be careful! In the beginning you may fully intend to stop the gossip; but it's very easy to be seduced into enjoying it yourself.

Dr. Michael Sedler suggests that we ask our friends a question or two to thwart a conversation that's turning toward gossip. Some examples include:

- "Is this something I need to hear about?"
- "What specific parts of this conversation need to be discussed with me?"
- "Who told you this information?"
- "Have you spoken with those people who are directly involved in this situation?"[4]

The key is to be gentle yet firm in our approach, also recognizing the same tact may need to be taken with us sometime. Confrontation can be difficult, especially with people we care about. But remember this: "My brethren, if any among you strays from the truth and one turns him back, let him know that he who turns a sinner from the error of his way will save his soul from death and will cover a multitude of sins" (James 5:19–20).

Ask

Do I often resort to talking about other people when I am with friends?

How can I redirect a conversation when it turns to gossip?

Dear Lord, Help me this week to more closely examine my conversations. Search my heart and show me any impure motives for spreading gossip. Give me the wisdom and courage to stop it when I hear it. In Jesus' Name, Amen.

by Pamela Anderson

WHITEWASHED *Tombs*

Woe to you, teachers of the law and Pharisees, you hypocrites! You are like whitewashed tombs, which look beautiful on the outside but on the inside are full of dead men's bones and everything unclean. In the same way, on the outside you appear to people as righteous but on the inside you are full of hypocrisy and wickedness.
MATTHEW 23:27–28 NIV

★ ★ ★

AS A MILITARY WIFE, I have moved several times over the past few years, as have many of you. For me this constantly mobile lifestyle has, at times, made getting into a regular housecleaning "groove" a struggle, so at our last duty station I decided to conquer my haphazard cleaning routine once and for all.

The first day using a new cleaning system, I was a domestic diva. By 10:00 a.m. all rooms had been straightened, the kitchen floor swept, laundry started, all bathroom sinks were gleaming. The next day, I set about completing my daily household chores with even more fervor.

On that particular morning a furniture repairman arrived to fix a spring in our couch. I proudly led him through shining halls to the living room. However, my smug satisfaction turned suddenly to horror when the repairman flipped the couch over. Writhing, slimy bugs of every size slithered and scampered over a moldy ice cream carton.

Later, after all the bugs had been killed, vacuumed up,

and the repairman sent on his way, I pondered the lesson of the writhing, slimy bugs. I had cleaned and straightened the surface of my home, but had neglected the dust bunnies under the beds and the pestilence under the couch. In the previous Scripture passage Jesus is upbraiding the Pharisees for trying this same surface approach regarding righteousness. They labored hard to say and do those things that would cause them to appear righteous, but Jesus could see their true inner motivations. He could see each instance of hypocrisy and wickedness, each writhing and slimy bug.

Sadly, I know that I, too, am guilty of surface cleaning my heart, of trying to whitewash a tomb of hidden and unrepented sin. But there is no shortcut to true righteousness. Psalm 51 records David's words after he was confronted by the prophet Nathan for his adulterous affair with Bathsheba. Verses 6 and 7 read, "Behold, You desire truth in the innermost being, and in the hidden part You will make me know wisdom. Purify me with hyssop and I shall be clean." David thought he had adequately whitewashed his sin by manipulating circumstances, but the truth was never hidden from God's eyes. Our heavenly Father requires integrity at every level. He is never concerned with how things look, but with how they really are. David's "whitewashed tomb" literally contained a dead man's bones, those of Bathsheba's husband, Uriah. What's in yours?

Ask

Am I more concerned with how things look
than with how they really are?
Is there an area of my life that I have tried to whitewash
before God to avoid dealing with hidden sins?

Pray

Dear Lord, I confess to You that in the past I have tried to hide my guilt by merely surface cleaning my heart and neglecting the hidden sins I think no one can see. I repent of my hypocrisy and wickedness and choose instead to pursue truth in the inmost places of my soul and mind. Teach me Your wisdom, cleanse me, wash me. Let me not be a whitewashed tomb full of every unclean thing, but rather let me be a woman of integrity pure and righteous, without and within. In Jesus' Name, Amen.

by Jocelyn Green

TAMING *Jealousy*

Rejoice with those who rejoice,
and weep with those who weep.
ROMANS 12:15

★ ★ ★

AN AMAZING TRANSFORMATION took place among several of the Coast Guard wives in our unit when one Coastie was permitted to stay home and take care of his pregnant wife, who had recently broken her ankle in a car accident, while the rest of the husbands went underway (out to sea). These women had been worn raw with surprise trips throughout the year that took their other halves away from them. And now, when one husband stayed home, they became consumed with jealousy.

She isn't hurt that badly! He doesn't have to take care of her—he's just lazy. Nobody else wants to go on this patrol either, but you don't see them staying home! The more these women vented to each other, the more intense their jealousy became. Soon, this couple had become a scapegoat. Bitter words turned into bitter behavior as women deliberately shunned them as some sort of futile protest.

James says, "For where jealousy and selfish ambition exist, there is disorder and every evil thing" (James 3:16). There was certainly disorder in the hearts of the jealous women, and as a result, there was disorder in the entire Coast Guard community for weeks.

Most of the material I have read about jealousy and envy deals with an unabated desire for things. While I'm sure we can all relate to that struggle, it seems to me that the military wife is even more prone to being jealous over how others are treated compared to us, or how and with whom others can spend their time. But Paul tells us to "Rejoice with those who rejoice, and weep with those who weep" (Romans 12:15).

In Matthew 20, Jesus shares the parable of the laborers in the vineyard. In this story, a landowner goes out five times throughout the day, from early morning to the eleventh hour, to hire men to work in his vineyard. When the men were paid their wages at the end of the day, those who had worked all day complained not that their wages were unfair, but that those who had worked only one hour were paid the same amount. The landowner responded by saying, "Take what is yours and go, but I wish to give to this last man the same as to you. Is it not lawful for me to do what I wish with what is my own? Or is your eye envious because I am generous?" (Matthew 20:14–15).

The grumbling workers were not satisfied with their provision because they focused instead on what others received. In the same way, when we shift our focus from God's provision for us and look at the provisions of others, we are naturally going to draw comparisons that are not always positive. In the military lifestyle, there will always be people around us in both tougher and easier circumstances. Let us be content with how God provides for us and not stew in our jealousy over a situation we cannot control.

Ask

Am I harboring jealousy for someone else's belongings or circumstance? If I didn't know about the above example, would I be more content with my lot in life?

Lord, Purge my heart of all unselfishness so that I can truly rejoice with those who rejoice and weep with those who weep. Instead of comparing my life to everyone else's, help me be content in Your provision and trust that whatever I need, You will supply. In Jesus' Name, Amen.

by Jocelyn Green

ASKING FOR *Help*

For when I am weak, then I am strong.
2 CORINTHIANS 12:10

★ ★ ★

THE WEEKLY BIBLE STUDY I hosted in my home was two hours away and my driveway was buried in snow. It needed to be cleared before people arrived.

I could just start shoveling, I told myself. But before my husband went underway, he had said, "Remember, if you need anything, the EO [engineering officer] is staying home this time. If it snows, he can plow out the driveway for you." But I had never asked anyone for help when my husband was at sea before.

Once I finally asked the EO to plow me out, the job was done in about ten minutes. I was ashamed of myself for needing to beat back my pride and allow someone else to help me.

We are called military "dependents," and yet we have to be extremely independent when our husbands are off serving the country. It's fitting for us to be self-confident and competent women, ready to tackle the obstacles that crop up in our path. We wouldn't survive otherwise! But I discovered that I was becoming overly self-reliant. In an effort to not appear "weak," I was unwilling to humbly admit that I couldn't do everything in my own strength. Pride was stealthily taking root in my heart.

There are times in every military wife's life when she could use a helping hand—whether or not she wants to admit it and actually ask for it. Paul had the opposite point of view. "Therefore

I am well content with weaknesses, with insults, with distresses, with persecutions, with difficulties, for Christ's sake; for when I am weak, then I am strong" (2 Corinthians 12:10). When we are weak, Christ can take over for us and give us His strength, glorifying His name in the process.

We need to humbly invite God to enable us to live through His power (Philippians 4:13), and the way that we do that is by staying connected to Him as the vine, the source of life. "I am the vine, you are the branches; he who abides in Me, and I in him, he bears much fruit, for apart from Me you can do nothing" (John 15:5). If we were to cut ourselves off from the vine in order to prove just how independent we were, it would spell certain death for us.

We also must recognize that when we ask for help from God, he often meets our needs through the community around us. Most people are eager to help—I bet you are the same way. How often have we thought, *I wish there was something I could do for that family*, but didn't follow through because we didn't know what to do? Nothing will happen unless you let the people around you know your specific needs. When you do ask God and your community for support, you will be amazed at the blessings that have been waiting for you!

Ask

Is my reluctance to ask for help a sign of pride in my own self-reliance?
Is there something I could be asking for help with this week?

Pray

Lord, Forgive me if I have been trying to live life so much in my own strength that I have been denying You the chance to fill me with Yours. Remind me daily that You are the vine, I am the branch. Without You, I cannot live. Show me how You'd like to bless me through my community, and give me the humility to ask for help. In Jesus' Name, Amen.

Section Three

AMBASSADORS FOR CHRIST:

Viewing Our Role as a Ministry

Whatever you do in word or deed,
do all in the name of the Lord Jesus, giving thanks
through Him to God the Father.

COLOSSIANS 3:17

By Denise McColl

AND YOU SHALL BE MY *Witnesses...*

You will receive power when the Holy Spirit has come upon you; and you shall be My witnesses both in Jerusalem, and in all Judea and Samaria, and even to the remotest part of the earth.
ACTS 1:8

★ ★ ★

HAVE YOU EVER THOUGHT of your military "assignments" as avenues of opportunity to be His witness "to the ends of the earth"? Wow! That sure puts a positive spin on places we "have to go" or "thought we'd never find ourselves." I didn't always have that optimistic outlook. I came into the military (by marriage to my husband) with a good bit of a kick and a spit. I remember being so deeply in love with my debonair Navy submariner that I accepted the time he had to pay back in Naval service for the education he had received from the Naval Academy. It was a requirement; I would merely endure four years.

At this point, after twenty-two years of service, I humbly admit my shame in my initial unwillingness to take my place as a soldier for Christ in the group of larger soldiers serving in our nation's armed forces. In His persistent time, He has turned my ungratefulness into undying gratitude, revealing to me the *privilege* of our military mission, not the imposition of it. I am humbled to realize that He actually chose us for this honorable place of acting as mobile missionaries.

During what I thought was our most challenging assignment yet (Guam), God began the chiseling and remodeling of my heart that I thought was already well under way. So much did He impassion me with the things that impassioned Him that He inspired the writing of *Footsteps of the Faithful* in which I shared much of His work of molding me as a usable vessel, while supporting my husband's Navy service. Funny how God's work shines the brightest in the darkest of places! Once I began working with instead of against Him, He enabled me to turn obstacles into opportunities. And oh, the deep satisfaction that came from seizing those chances to share the grace and guidance of Christ with the many people around us.

The military mission field is ever changing, fresh, and vibrant. What a joy it continues to be to watch seeds planted, watered, and grown to fruition as He ovesees the ripening harvest. God's passion is people, and so ours should be! Where will be your next Judea, Samaria? Take up your cross with Him wherever He leads. And take comfort, too, in the knowledge that He accompanies you, even precedes you as His work never ceases to be made manifest all over the world. "Go therefore and make disciples of all the nations . . . teaching them to observe all that I commanded you; and lo, I am with you always, even to the end of the age" (Matthew 28:19, 20).

Ask

Am I fulfilling my commission as a military service member but omitting His greater commission to spread His healing mercy and purpose to a military world in need of Christ? Am I going through the motions of duty and moving rather than looking at each assignment as a new Judea or Samaria?

Lord, Reignite my desire to serve You as I move about. Create in me an excitement, an anticipation about each new assignment, deployment, tour of duty, that I might be ready "in and out of season" to share the hope that is in You. Give me zeal for the Judeas and Samarias you put before me as places with incredible potential to be an ambassador for You. In Jesus' Name, Amen.

by Jill Hart

God's REPRESENTATIVE

And whatever you do, whether in word or deed,
do it all in the name of the Lord Jesus, giving thanks
to God the Father through him.
COLOSSIANS 3:17 NIV

★ ★ ★

GOING FROM CIVILIAN LIFE to being a military wife, I found that I had a lot to learn. The rules on base differed greatly from the rules I was used to. For example, one of the hardest changes for me was driving 35 miles per hour everywhere I went on base. It was a big adjustment for me to go from carefree twenty-something to ultra-careful, non-speeding wife. However, I knew that everything I did now reflected not only on me, but on my husband as well. I had to get used to the fact that as an airman's wife, I represented him—especially when interacting with others on base.

This is true of us as Christians as well. Our words and actions represent Jesus to others. It's humbling to think that our interaction with someone who knows of our faith could have an eternal impact on their life. The question is, how do we best reflect the love of Christ?

The religious leaders of Jesus' time wondered this as well. They wanted Jesus to tell them which of their hundreds of religious laws was most important, which would give them the highest standing in God's eyes. But He surprised them. He replied: " 'Love the Lord your God with all your heart and with all your soul and with all your mind.' This is the first and greatest commandment. And the second is like it: 'Love your neighbor as yourself' " (Matthew 22:37–38 NIV).

It almost seems too simple, doesn't it? To best reflect our Savior's love, we're to do two things:

1. Love God above all else, with every fiber of our being.
2. Love those around us.

What this looks like in practice will be different in each of our lives. However, we have the perfect example in Christ. We can read the Bible anytime for stories and examples of how Jesus handled friendships, enemies, and even a death that He didn't deserve.

So next time you wonder if others are seeing God's love reflected in your life, take a moment to evaluate how you're doing in each of the two areas. Are you putting God first at work, in your marriage, in parenting, in other areas of your day-to-day life? Are you loving others, putting their needs ahead of your own? What about those who may not be so easy to love? Are you showing kindness to the annoying neighbor, the pushy sales clerk, and the obnoxious teenager at chapel?

Ask

How am I showing my love for the Lord?
In what ways can I reach out to others,
even those who aren't easy to love?

Pray

Dear Lord, You've told us that the two most important acts for us as Your children are to love You and love others. Please show me how I can reach out to those around me as a testimony to Your love. Please help me to strive to please You above all others and to keep my life focused on You. In Jesus' Name, Amen.

by Vanessa Peters

Eyes WIDE OPEN

The King will reply, "I tell you the truth, whatever you did for one of the least of these brothers of mine, you did for me."
MATTHEW 25:40 NIV

★ ★ ★

IN ALL THE PLACES we've lived during our years in the military, we've noticed a theme among many of the "locals." Particularly for the young people, the world is not much bigger than their immediate circle. It may be their high school, or church, city, or even their state. Even with some adults, it's as though the world at large doesn't exist. Maybe it's because the sufferings of others around the world are too much to bear. Or maybe it stems from complete self-absorption. In any case, it's an issue worth addressing, and seeking what the Bible has to say about it:

"How true it is that God does not show favoritism but accepts men from every nation who fear him and do what is right" (Acts 10:34–35 NIV).

"As believers in our glorious Lord Jesus Christ, don't show favoritism. . . . Has not God chosen those who are poor in the eyes of the world to be rich in faith and to inherit the kingdom He promised those who love Him? (James 2:1, 5 NIV).

While it's natural to congregate with others like us, Christians should not pick favorites. Furthermore, God wants us to witness to those in our community, country, and the rest of the world.

One place where we lived had a literal "other side of the

tracks." Folks on the west side just didn't associate with lower-income folks from the east side, and vice versa. Then the opportunity came for me to mentor a young mom from the east side through a crisis pregnancy center's "Earn While You Learn" program. It was fantastic! How thankful I was to the Lord not only for this sweet new friendship, but for the way my eyes were opened to the life of this family separated not by distance, but by social and economic class.

The eleven disciples, all of Jewish descent, were asked to make disciples of *all* nations. The charge for us is no different. As disciples of Jesus, we are called to live a life of outreach. Sometimes, we're surprised by the mission field all around us. Other times, we step out in faith to minister cross-culturally overseas. Either way, God will provide opportunities if we seek with willing hearts.

It's great to associate with other military families, since we have a lot in common and can share one another's burdens. But what if we found even greater blessings in reaching outside our exclusive comfort zones and looking for people of other races, classes, and careers to befriend? Open your eyes and heart to follow God's calling to the least of these all around us.

Ask

Do I willingly reach outside my own comfort zone?
Where could I invest myself to reach the least of these,
or just folks who are different than me?

Pray

Father, Help me to love all Your children as You do. Stretch my faith and character through interaction and friendship with people of varying backgrounds and stations in life. In Jesus' Name, Amen.

by Jill Hart

Reaching Out, Changing *Lives*

For I was hungry and you gave me something to eat,
I was thirsty and you gave me something to drink,
I was a stranger and you invited me in, I needed clothes
and you clothed me, I was sick and you looked after me,
I was in prison and you came to visit me.
Matthew 25:35–36 NIV

★ ★ ★

As my daughter's friends began arriving for her birthday party, I noticed one girl, Sarah, clinging to her mom and begging her to stay. I could see the tears welling up in her eyes as she watched her mom walk back to their car.

Sarah remained quiet all afternoon. After the party, Sarah and Kaitlyn played quietly in Kaitlyn's room. I was proud to see Kaitlyn being sensitive to her feelings and making an extra effort to be kind to her.

When Major Smith arrived, we were surprised to find that Sarah didn't want to leave. As we sat in the living room and chatted, giving the girls some additional time to play, she opened up about her daughter's behavior. "I just returned from a six-month deployment in Iraq. Sarah lives in constant fear that I'll leave her again."

Perhaps you know someone who is deployed and had to leave their children behind, or a lonely neighbor whose spouse is overseas. How can you make a difference in their lives? Make a list of ways that you can reach out to the families of those deployed:

1. Pray regularly for them.
2. Provide an hour or two of childcare to allow them some time of their own.
3. Locate a local organization such as Operation Voices and Love (http://www.operationvoicesandlove.com/) to bless the children with a teddy bear containing a voice message from their deployed parent.
4. Invite them over for a meal.
5. ______________________________
6. ______________________________
7. ______________________________
8. ______________________________
9. ______________________________
10. ______________________________

We see a powerful example of God's command to us to care for others in Matthew 25:34–40 NIV.

> "Then the King will say to those on his right, 'Come, you who are blessed by my Father; take your inheritance, the kingdom prepared for you since the creation of the world. For I was hungry and you gave me something to eat, I was thirsty and you gave me something to drink, I was a stranger and you invited me in, I needed clothes and you clothed me, I was sick and you looked after me, I was in prison and you came to visit me.'
>
> "Then the righteous will answer him, 'Lord, when did we see you hungry and feed you, or thirsty and give you something to drink? When did we see you a stranger and invite you in, or needing clothes and clothe you? When did we see you sick or in prison and go to visit you?'
>
> "The King will reply, 'I tell you the truth, whatever you did for one of the least of these brothers of mine, you did for me.'"

In the same way, when we reach out to families of those who are deployed, we are obeying Christ's command to meet each other's needs.

Ask

Who do I know that I can reach out to?
How can I get others involved that would like to help me support these families?

Pray

Dear Lord, Thank you for the men and women serving our country and sacrificing time away from their families to do so. Please bless them richly. Please show me how to serve those around me and help me find ways to reach out to those in need. In Jesus' Name, Amen.

by Jocelyn Green

EVERY NATION, UNDER *God*

And they sang a new song, saying, "Worthy are You to take the book and to break its seals; for You were slain, and purchased for God with Your blood men from every tribe and tongue and people and nation. You have made them to be a kingdom and priests to our God; and they will reign upon the earth."

REVELATION 5:9–10

★ ★ ★

IF ANYONE KNOWS THE MEANING OF PATRIOTISM, military families do. An unhealthy measure of patriotic pride, however, is misleading and even unbiblical.

Allow me to share an example. One year, my husband and I attended an Easter morning church service in a major Navy city on the East Coast. Near the beginning of the service, children paraded toward the cross at the front of the sanctuary, each holding a small flag representing a different country. Then a trumpet sounded, and a military officer in dress whites walked down the aisle alone, carrying a full-size American flag. The congregation erupted into applause, which lasted from the first sight of the flag to the moment the officer was seated.

The officer towered over the children, implying that even at the foot of the cross, all nations are not equal. The congregation's reaction to the symbol of the cross was not nearly as profound as its reaction to the symbol of the United States flag.

While this particular church's display does not represent every church's attitude, let it be a warning to us. We must remember that in God's eyes, every nation is equal. We must remember that Christianity is not exclusively an American religion, but that we have bold brothers and sisters in Christ all over the world.

Paul's letter to the Galatians reminds us all that our first allegiance, and the primary source of our identity, is to Christ. "There is neither Jew nor Greek, there is neither slave nor free man, there is neither male nor female; for you are all one in Christ Jesus" (Galatians 3:28). To the Philippians, Paul wrote, "For our citizenship is in heaven" (Philippians 3:20). The message is clear. No matter how much we love our country, we should never place loyalty to it over loyalty to Christ. Even before we are Americans (or Africans, or Latin Americans, or Asians), we are Christians.

When does my patriotism begin to look like an idol—
that is, something that is placed before Christ?
How can I learn more about my fellow Christians
in other countries?

Pray

Dear Lord, Thank You for allowing me to live and serve in the United States of America. Show me how to maintain a healthy patriotism for the country You have placed me in without succumbing to the idea that Americans are superior to other nations. I praise You for purchasing with Your blood people from every tribe and tongue and nation. Please help me develop a heart for learning about and praying for my brothers and sisters around the world. In Jesus' Name, Amen.

by Denise McColl

THE *Jonah* IN ALL OF US

Beloved, let us love one another, for love is from God, and everyone who loves is born of God and knows God.
1 JOHN 4:7

★ ★ ★

ONE AREA WHERE WE OFTEN GET CAUGHT tweaking and just plain "trying too hard" is the subtle way we strive to build relationships predominantly within the civilian community, to guard against the pain of losing friendships with military folks who inevitably move on. We've thought about it, maybe even tried it—it's a natural self-protection to help minimize the many variables of this nomadic sort of life. In my younger days as a Navy wife, I remember trying this very self-protective plan myself. It took God a firm tugging at the heart to reach me, but get through He did.

"These are all people who matter to me," came His clear, gentle persuasion. His careful chiseling began opening my closed, hardened heart to replace it with one that cared more about "them" than "myself." "The fact is, Denise, you don't know the gems I have for you behind any number of those closed doors. More important than that, there are scores of them who need to know Me, trust in Me, allow Me to guide them through this military maze. I've already imparted to all of you the importance of holding on to this world and its fragile securities ever so lightly. This world is not your real home, but rather a resting place here and there on the journey to your eternal home with Me. Doesn't that perspective make all of the moving and changes (even the relationships?) easier to handle? Don't be so quick to 'write off' those on your own team because you've 'had enough' or you're just tired of the whole military theme.

"Remember, this is a big part of your mission; this is what you took on when you agreed to serve your country in this way. Don't be like Jonah and run the other way. Not that I can't also use you with civilian friends. You remain willing, open, available, and I'll bless you with both! Don't forget those whom you push away are the volunteers, the called-out ones, those willing to sacrifice, yet many of them are marching out of sheer patriotism. Imagine what a joy it would be to see them march to My completely purposeful, satisfying, and fulfilling drumbeat as they serve to guard against evil around the world.

"Like a storm-tossed ship on Jonah's sea of self-centeredness, this could be the essence of your military experience. Could the military be your Ninevah? Trying to handpick your own friends and opportunities stifles My rich and abundant plan for your life. Remember, 'My thoughts are not your thoughts, neither are your ways my ways' (Isaiah 55:9). Also remember that My gifts are far more precious than anything you could search out for yourself. Stop running. Stop striving. Walk with me."

Ask

Am I running away from a greater plan God has for me
in not really wanting to get involved in relationships
within the military community?
Could I be missing out on His abundant gift of friendships
by not allowing myself to be available?

Pray

Lord, Help me to look beyond my small, limited, sometimes self-protecting plans to Your great and wonderful, matchless plans as I serve in the military. Help me to trust You with my relationships, allowing You to guide and direct those You allow in my life. Thank You for helping me not to miss out on Your precious gifts! In Jesus' Name, Amen.

by Jocelyn Green

Loving THE UNLIKELY

You have heard that it was said, "You shall love your neighbor and hate your enemy." But I say to you, love your enemies and pray for those who persecute you, so that you may be sons of your Father who is in heaven. . . . For if you love those who love you, what reward do you have?

MATTHEW 5:43–46

★ ★ ★

BEFORE I MARRIED INTO THE MILITARY, friendships were far less complicated. I could choose my own friends, and if I didn't have much in common with someone, I chose not to spend time with her. As an officer's wife, however, things were a little different. I regularly found myself in social situations with other officers' wives, and it was usually easy to befriend them—with one exception.

The work relationship between her husband and mine, the top two in command on the same Coast Guard cutter, could be described as rocky at best. She regularly told me how my husband could do his job better, which aggravated me to the point where I no longer wanted to spend time with her.

But as a Christian, I couldn't just cut her off. Jesus said to love our enemies and pray for those who persecute us. I was commanded to love her, regardless of how she made me feel, and regardless of how her husband treated mine. Plus, I was one of the only Christians she knew. I had a unique opportunity to represent Christ to her that should not be wasted.

You've probably been in the same situation. Perhaps you are there right now, knowing you need to love someone on your base or in your community that you just don't like. Maybe this person has hurt you or your family through word or deed. Whatever he or she has done, the commandment is the same: love.

We must love our enemies with *agape* love, a love that seeks nothing in return. Take a moment to examine yourself. Have you done anything, intentionally or not, to provoke their unfriendly treatment of you? Look for the good in that person in your life who seems very unlikable.

As difficult and unnatural as it sometimes feels, we can't get away from the commandment to love: our neighbor, our brother and sister, our enemy, and above all, the Lord our God with all our hearts, souls, and minds. 1 John 4:7–8 says, "Love is from God; and everyone who loves is born of God and knows God. The one who does not love does not know God, for God is love."

Ask

Who am I having a difficult time loving right now?
Am I doing anything to harm my Christian testimony because of it?

Pray

Dear Lord, You know it isn't natural for me to love ________. But I know You loved him/her enough to die for his/her salvation. Help me see the good that You see in him/her. Take away any desire on my part to see him/her fail. Please give me Your heart and Your love for this person, that I might be used of You for Your purposes. In Jesus' Name, Amen.

by Paulette L. Harris

FAMILY OF *God*

But He answered and said to them, "My mother and My brothers are those who hear the word of God and do it."
LUKE 8:21

★ ★ ★

SOBS CAME FROM THE OTHER END OF THE PHONE as my friend Ellen called from the military hospital. She was in the beginning stages of miscarrying her baby and couldn't get a hold of her husband who was temporarily assigned to another base.

When I arrived at the hospital, I was told that no one was allowed in except for close relatives. "But I am her sister," I protested to the nurse, reasoning that she was my spiritual sister. It worked. I rushed in to comfort Ellen as she broke into fresh sobs.

As a Christian woman, I did have some regrets about not telling the truth to the nurse on duty. I went to her after Ellen's husband arrived and explained what I had done and that I was sorry but wanted so much to help Ellen until her husband could be with her.

She laughed and said, "I knew it all the time; well, it's just that you two ladies do look so much alike that I didn't think anyone would ask anyway, and your sisterhood just seemed to be so natural."

Psalm 68:6 NIV says, "God sets the lonely in families." For those of us in the military, our families become our brothers and sisters in Christ since our flesh and blood families are rarely in close proximity. Those years in the military will always be special as we all learned how to take care of one another as God's family.

Jesus has always been faithful to prepare a spiritual family to greet us as we come into new places, even in retirement. God put us into a community of believers planted there that embraced us. As each family was transferred, our small group would begin to pray for a replacement family to come and help in loving and supporting one another in the body of Christ.

It is both our privilege and our responsibility to care for our fellow believers wherever we are. Besides being a priceless encouragement and support to one another, we are told to love each other because (1) God first loved us while we were yet in our sin (1 John 4:11); and (2) our love for each other marks us as disciples of Jesus (John 13:35).

We often remark about how there is no family like the military family. And while the bonds among fellow servicemen/women and their families are undoubtedly strong, they are even stronger—and sweeter—among followers of Christ. It's an honor to take care of each other!

Ask

Have you found a body of believers that you can minister Christ to and be loved and ministered to by them as you walk with Jesus? What does someone in your body need today that you can provide?

Pray

Father, I thank You for all the times that You take care of us. You provide family and friends when we need it the most. You really do care about the number of hairs on our heads and send just what we need when we need it. Thank You for the body of Christ, our family here to help us grow spiritually. Thank You that wherever You send us as we serve our country there will always be a family of believers. In Jesus' Name, Amen.

by Jocelyn Green

LOVING WHEN IT *Hurts*

A friend loves at all times, and a brother is born for adversity.
PROVERBS 17:17

★ ★ ★

I HAD ONLY BEEN A MILITARY WIFE for a few months before I made a conscious decision to not get attached to people in our new town of Homer, Alaska. Still reeling from the good-byes from our previous home of Washington, D.C., I was trying to safeguard myself against the pain that would inevitably come when it was time to move on again.

But then I met a woman in my Bible study who was battling breast cancer for the second time. When I brought her family a meal, I ended up talking with her for hours. She wanted to know who I was and what made me tick. Soon, I was driving her two hundred miles for her cancer treatments and back again. I hosted slumber parties for her and her daughter while Rob was at sea. When she said, "I love you," I responded likewise. In that instant, I knew that my plan of apathy had failed.

And it was all her fault. Here she was, battling for her life, and yet still dispensing love to me, a woman who would be gone in less than two years. If anyone had a right to reserve her love and attention for only her family, it was her. But if anything, knowing that her time on earth could be short spurred her on to love and pray for more people than ever before. I was humbled by the size of her heart and the stinginess of my own.

What if I find a kindred spirit who I will have to say good-bye to when our time here is up? I worried. But of course, the alternative would be even worse. If I never established lifelines there, would I somehow feel better about things?

Jesus told us to love our neighbor as ourselves (Matthew 22:39). He didn't say, "Love as long as you feel you have nothing to lose." He simply said, "Love."

John reminds us in 1 John 4:7–8, "Beloved, let us love one another, for love is from God, and everyone who loves is born of God and knows God. The one who does not love does not know God, for God is love."

Paul tells us in 1 Corinthians 13:2 that "if I have all faith, so as to remove mountains, but do not have love, I am nothing." He ends the chapter by saying love is greater than even faith and hope.

We need to love, even if it hurts. Loving is not a matter of feelings, it's fulfilling a commandment. While of course it's hard to part ways at the end of our assignments, think how much people enrich our lives in the meantime. We are not called to feel safe and comfortable all the time—we are called to be obedient. Lucky for us, that includes a commitment to loving people.

Ask

Am I holding myself back from being a part of someone's life? What can I do to show love to someone in my Bible study or neighborhood this week?

Pray

Lord, When I am tempted to protect myself by keeping my heart locked up inside of me, give me the strength to open up to the people You have already decided should be part of my life here. Show me how I can be an encouragement to others. May we take care of each other in such a way that others can tell we are Your disciples. In Jesus' Name, Amen.

by Vanessa Peters and Jocelyn Green

TAKING THE FIRST *Step*

Owe nothing to anyone except to love one another;
for he who loves his neighbor has fulfilled the law.
ROMANS 13:8

★ ★ ★

AS A MILITARY FAMILY new to the neighborhood and living off base for the first time, we were surprised that many of the neighbors failed to welcome us. "Crotchety old man," I (Vanessa) thought disapprovingly of one particular hermit. "What kind of neighbor didn't even respond to cheerful hellos?"

Then one day I reluctantly brought extra cookies to him. Surprised, he gladly accepted them and explained that he was the sole caregiver for his dying wife, who hadn't left her bed in more than two years.

A few days later I received the call from Mrs. Schroeder to come by and meet her. Oh, but I felt so unqualified to visit a deathbed and put off the visit until I could avoid it no longer. I dipped some strawberries in chocolate, grabbed my four-year-old for a quick escape if needed, and headed next door.

What I found in the next thirty minutes was a wonderful fulfillment of the Scripture that says that God's strength is made perfect in weakness. For it was He alone who filled me with His Spirit and allowed me to have an amazing visit with Mrs. Schroeder. We held hands, we laughed, and we prayed like we were old friends.

My visit to Mrs. Schroeder proved to be a blessing both to

her and to me. But it never would have happened if I hadn't taken that first step. While we as military wives would hope that our new neighbors would welcome us at every new location to ease the frequent transitions, sometimes we need to be the first ones reaching out.

Hospitality is a virtue based on the biblical principle of loving our neighbors as ourselves. It is the art of creating a generous, cordial, pleasant, or sustaining environment.[1] We often think of it in terms of having people over to our own homes. But you can bring the heart of hospitality with you wherever you go.

One definition of "hospitable" is "favoring the health, growth, comfort, etc., of new arrivals."[2] Chances are, you may be the new arrival on your block. But if your neighbors don't come to you first, take your hospitality with you when you leave the house—even if your neighbors seem unwelcoming to you.

In Matthew 5:46–47, Jesus says: "For if you love those who love you, what reward do you have? Do not even the tax collectors do the same? If you greet only your brothers, what more are you doing than others? Do not even the Gentiles do the same?"

And just a little later, in Matthew 7:12, he says: "In everything, therefore, treat people the same way you want them to treat you, for this is the Law and the Prophets." Do you wish your neighbors would introduce themselves to you? Go on over and start the introductions. Do you wish your block would have parties like you've enjoyed before? Throw one yourself.

Ask

Are there unlovable folks around me that I could reach out to?
Has anyone specifically been on my heart lately?
What can I do for a neighbor this week?

Father, It is difficult to love those who are different than I am. Yet, I know that each human is a soul created in Your own image. Help me to love recklessly and be a risk taker when it comes to reaching out and relationships. Take my eyes off myself so I will be able to focus on others! In Jesus' Name, Amen.

by Vanessa Peters

SEEKING SPIRITUAL *Food*

For everyone who partakes only of milk is not accustomed to the word of righteousness, for he is an infant. But solid food is for the mature, who because of practice have their senses trained to discern good and evil.
HEBREWS 5:13–14

★ ★ ★

TODAY I ATE THREE KRISPY KREME DONUTS and a large soda for lunch. While it tasted good, it didn't leave me feeling satisfied. Instead of being energized, I felt weighed down and drowsy. The initial sugar high did not last long, and short-term satisfaction replaced a more deeply filling, healthy choice.

This experience made me think about our recent search for a home church. Having recently PCS'd (Permanent Change of Station), my family visited many churches during a period of several weeks. While they all had friendly faces to welcome us, we came to realize that the sugary sweetness of a church that sometimes functions more like a social club must not replace real spiritual food.

From vague, pop culture church signs like "Respect others" and "Hold your wife and kids" to sermons including more jokes than Scripture, our experiences caused us to reevaluate what's really valuable in a church. Even better, it drove us to the Bible to determine what God has to say about meeting together in fellowship with other believers. As a military family facing continual relocation, these principles are essential to spiritual growth: "They were continually devoting themselves to the apostles' teaching and to fellowship, to the breaking of bread and to prayer" (Acts 2:42).

This early church example teaches us about the importance of fellowship and even what to look for in a church. First, we should make it a priority to fellowship with other believers somewhere. I've known discouraged Christians who decide to "do their own thing" on Sunday morning, but Scripture commands us to do otherwise (see also Hebrews 10:25). Second, find a congregation that prays earnestly and gives generously—and encourages its members to do likewise. Third, we need to seek a church where we are free to truly praise God. If church leaders do not cultivate a heart of worship, we need to reconsider. Finally, we should be attending churches that are "adding to their number . . . those who [are] being saved" (Acts 2:47). The church we choose should passionately grow more Christ-followers—and we should be a part of that!

Furthermore, we join a new church with the intention of sharing our spiritual gifts: "When you come together, everyone has a [gift]. . . . All of these must be done for the strengthening of the church" (1 Corinthians 14:26 NIV). In today's consumer culture, many folks go "church shopping" to find one that best meets their family's needs. While some of those points are valid, we must also be concerned with how our gifts can strengthen a church where God may place us.

Next time you PCS, don't settle for Krispy Kremes and soda, or as the Bible puts it, "spiritual milk." Look for the rich, solid food that leads to righteousness, maturity, and satisfaction.

Ask

What criteria does my family hold for
deciding on a new church when we move?
Am I actively seeking ways to bless the fellowship of believers
with my own spiritual gifts?

Pray

Lord Jesus, We want to be plugged in to a group of Christians who are passionate about Your glory and the lost. As we move from base to base, give us spiritual eyes to see where You would have us grow and invest our gifts. In Jesus' Name, Amen.

by Jocelyn Green

Branded

I bear on my body the brand-marks of Jesus.
GALATIANS 6:17

★ ★ ★

"HI, I'M JOCELYN." I was one of several new Coast Guard wives being welcomed to the unit with a potluck luncheon. Already unsure of myself in this new military world, I was completely taken aback when my introduction of myself was countered with, "Oh, don't bother telling us your name. You're the XO's wife, and that's all you'll ever be to us." She then suggested that she would buy a T-shirt for me emblazoned with "XO's wife" so no one would ever need to wonder.

My husband's title had just branded me for the duration of my time in this tiny town of Homer, Alaska. Perhaps I should have expected it, but I was frustrated. I wanted to be identified for who I was, not for what Rob did for a living.

And then I realized something else: instead of seeking to declare my identity as an individual, I really should have been more concerned with staking my identity in Christ. What truly matters is who I am—who we are— *in Christ.*

National Guard wife Amy MacLeod says, "Although it is not always easy, I must see myself through the lens of Jesus. His blood has washed me, and I am a new creation (2 Corinthians 5:17) fully pleasing to God. I am loved by God with a love that surpasses knowledge (Ephesians 3:18, 19). I am beautiful because a holy, perfect God formed me in my mother's womb

(Psalm 139:15). I am strong because the same Spirit that raised Christ from the dead dwells in me (Romans 8:11). I can do all things through Christ who strengthens me (Philippians 4:13). I have a purpose (Ephesians 2:10), and I am well equipped for the task (2 Timothy 3:16, 17)."

Our goal should be to be so firm in our identity with Christ that our love and service for him is unmistakable to those who see us. Exodus 21 says that if, at the end of six years, a Hebrew slave decides he loves his master and chooses not to be set free, "then his master shall bring him to God, then he shall bring him to the door or the doorpost. And his master shall pierce his ear with an awl; and he shall serve him permanently" (verse 6). The pierced ear identified him as a bondslave for the rest of his life. It was a reminder both to himself and to all who met him.

When Paul says in Galatians 6:17 that he bears brand-marks for Jesus, some theologians say he is identifying himself as Christ's willing bondslave for life. No matter who we are, where we are stationed, or what our husbands do in service for our country, may we strive to make our most defining, identifiable characteristic that of willing service to Jesus Christ.

Ask

Where do I place my identity right now?
Even if people knew little else about me,
would they be able to tell I am a servant of Jesus?

Pray

Lord, Help me to be firmly rooted in who You say I am. Let me not seek praise for myself or recognition for my own accomplishments, but may everything I say and do honor You. I am your willing bondslave; I never want to be set free from Your saving grace. In Jesus' Name, Amen.

by Ronda Sturgill

Moving: A MISSIONARY JOURNEY

Many are the plans in a man's heart,
but it is the Lord's purpose that prevails.
PROVERBS 19:21

★ ★ ★

WE HAD IT ALL PLANNED. We were going to stay in Virginia where our son was a junior at Virginia Commonwealth University in Richmond. We had just built the perfect wheelchair-accessible house, and we were within driving distance from my parents. Life was perfect . . . until we got orders to Davis-Monthan AFB in Tucson, Arizona.

"We're not moving to Tucson, Arizona!" I cried.

Three months later we were on our way. I know my claw marks are still embedded in the concrete of the interstate roads on which we traveled. My body was going to Tucson, but my heart was still in Virginia.

In the midst of my pain, God began to reveal to me why we were sent to this specific location. He brought me here to jump-start the dwindling Protestant Women of the Chapel (PWOC). In addition to myself, God brought some very special people to work along with me and before we knew it, the PWOC began to grow tremendously in both depth and breadth. In two years this ministry has become a beacon of God's light and love to many hurting military spouses. Also during this assignment, I was selected to be the PWOC West Region Coordinator, a position that oversees the local PWOCs at each military installation in the West. Through this position I've traveled all around the country, ministering to the wives of our active-duty military personnel.

Jeremiah 17:9 (NIV) says, "The heart is deceitful above all things and beyond cure. Who can understand it?" Our own hearts don't even know what is best for us. Scripture repeatedly tells us that for those who know God, our lives are continually being directed by God. "I know, O Lord, that a man's life is not his own; it is not for man to direct his steps" (Jeremiah 10:23). I pray this truth has been seared into my heart. Never again will I question our assignment.

I'm also reminded of Saul and Barnabus as they embarked on their first missionary journey. Acts 13:3–4 tells us, "After they [the church] had fasted and prayed, they placed their hands on them and sent them off. The two of them, sent on their way by the Holy Spirit, went down to Seleucia and sailed from there to Cyprus." As children of God we must believe that ultimately the Holy Spirit also, leads us from one location to the next.

God knows exactly what His purposes are for our lives so much better than we. He knows where He wants to send us, with whom He wants us to serve, and what He wants to accomplish through us at each location. Ladies, don't resist the next time you find out your assignment, is the last place you want to go. Trust God, embrace the assignment, and watch Him do amazing things.

Do I try to manipulate the assignment system,
or do I allow God to lead?
How have I embraced each assignment as God's will
for our lives?
What are the amazing things God has done at each assignment?

Pray

Dear Lord, Help me to accept each military assignment as an assignment from You. I know You have a special plan for us at each location. As You reveal Your purposes for my family, help me to embrace them wholeheartedly. I will give You all the praise and honor as I watch You do incredible things. In Jesus' Name, Amen.

Section Four

TAKING ORDERS:

Living the Life That Has Been Set before Us

Therefore, since we have so great a cloud of witnesses surrounding us, let us also lay aside every encumbrance and the sin which so easily entangles us, and let us run with endurance the race that is set before us.

HEBREWS 12:1

by Jocelyn Green

ACCEPTING YOUR *Assignment*

Let us also lay aside every encumbrance and the sin which so easily entangles us, and let us run with endurance the race that is set before us, fixing our eyes on Jesus.
HEBREWS 12:1–2

★ ★ ★

WHILE YOUR HUSBAND'S MILITARY ASSIGNMENTS are clearly spelled out in his transfer orders, your assignment can be found in a different document: your marriage certificate. Have you considered that as long as your husband is in the military, your own specific role of military wife is no less important than his?

Of course, your assignment is no less trying, either. I've heard many active-duty husbands say they are convinced that holding down the home front is the more difficult assignment. That may be true; but when wives can't move past their own hardships, the entire family suffers.

"Many military wives see themselves as 'victims' of their husband's career," says Air Force wife Patti Morse. "We need to accept our circumstances from God, trusting that He unerringly knows what is best for us. We need to move from the attitude of victim to an attitude of stewardship. We need to ask, 'God, how can I use my difficult circumstance or disability to serve You and to glorify You?'"

Linda Dillow says: "If we want to be women of contentment, we must choose to accept our portion, our assigned roles from God. We must make the choice to dwell on the positive aspects of our role in life. If we don't, we'll be discontent, always wanting something different from what we've been given."[1]

According to 1 Corinthians 4:2, "it is required of stewards that one be found trustworthy." If we are Christians who believe God is sovereign over all, we can believe that our assigned role as military wife has been entrusted to us by God. We can squander the opportunities that come with this assignment or, as a good steward, we can make the most out of them for the glory of God. We are in a unique position to minister to our husbands, our children, and other military families. I hope we can all echo National Guard wife Amy MacLeod when she says, "I am called to be a military wife. God knew I could do it when He gave me the assignment."

Ask

Do I tend to see myself more as a victim
or as a steward of my role?
What positive aspects about being a military wife
can I dwell on this week?

Pray

Lord, Give me Your perspective on my life. I don't want to miss anything You would have for me—help me to be faithful in the little things so I can prove faithful with much (Luke 16:10). Train my eyes to get off myself and look for ways to love others. Show me the ministry you want me to have in this stage of my life, and instill in my heart an abiding sense of purpose for my assignment as a military wife. In Jesus' Name, Amen.

by Vanessa Peters

NOTHING BUT A *Breath*

Man is like a breath; his days are like a fleeting shadow.
PSALM 144:4 NIV

★ ★ ★

SEPTEMBER 7, 2004. It was the day before my husband deployed to the Middle East. I had two young children who were really going to miss their daddy, and I already felt lost thinking about the impending separation from my true companion.

It was the best and worst of days. A friend kept the children so we could have one last romantic night together. We went to a small beach town to stay at a bed and breakfast. We shared a lovely dinner and took a long walk. It was a perfect night, but for the sinking feeling in my stomach.

We happened upon an old church with an attached cemetery. We read tombstone after tombstone. "Beloved Wife and Mother." "Pilot—1859." As I thought about all the lives they represented in just one specific location, I was suddenly struck by the brevity of life. So what should I do with my short time, and how do I respond to trials—like seeing my husband and children's father go off to war?

My thoughts wandered back to a conversation I had with my mentor, when I called her in tears about the deployment. "Well," she said, "you can choose to live to survive . . . or you can survive—so you can really live." I thought about what that meant. Am I here just to "make it through" and enjoy whatever pleasures can be found in mortal life? Not according to Solomon: "When I surveyed all that my hands had done and what I had toiled to achieve, everything was meaningless . . ." (Ecclesiastes 2:11 NIV). If all things are meaningless, what does it mean to "really live"? And how do I truly "live" when part of my life is missing?

Later, I recorded some of the answers that God spoke to my heart:

"Mine is just one lowly life that will soon fade into history. So for what and whom do I toil and strive though the difficult times? I strive in this world because I am created for the next— when my true identity will be fulfilled. And not just for a 'breath,' but for all eternity."

Reflecting on these truths, I was brought back to the reality that even though my husband is a gift from the Lord, my life is not only about him. My life with him is merely a transitional period to reach my true home. "But our citizenship is in heaven" (Philippians 3:20 NIV).

Like other people's, my life is filled with mountaintops and valleys. Instead of despairing, I look to become more like Christ and prepare for eternity. When the days of deployment seem long, I think on a day when there will be no more mourning, crying, or pain (Revelation 21:4). When the struggles of rearing young children alone seem overwhelming, I offer my work unto the Lord, remembering that I will "receive an inheritance as a reward" (Colossians 3:24 NIV). And when I feel alone, I close my eyes and picture myself surrounded in glory—never more loved, at home, and at peace in a place where I was meant to be all along.

Ask

What is keeping me from having a godly perspective during this deployment?

What can I do to encourage spiritual growth?

Pray

Father, I need You to be my husband when I'm separated from my spouse. Give me the strength to look forward to heaven when I face trials. In Jesus' Name, Amen.

by Jocelyn Green

THE FIRST *Call*

Be anxious for nothing, but in everything by prayer and supplication with thanksgiving let your requests be made known to God.
PHILIPPIANS 4:6

★ ★ ★

IN EVERY PLACE I HAVE LIVED, I have had at least one go-to friend to call on whenever I needed support, advice, or companionship—especially during those times when my husband was at sea or gone for training of some kind. I began to suspect my priorities were out of line when instead of letting my requests be known to God, the One who actually has the power to take care of my problems, I made them known to my friends first. My reliance on God was morphing into a reliance on my friends—a dangerous and unhealthy shift. I was missing out on the comfort only God can provide.

Jesus pulled away from His disciples at times and sought quiet communion with the heavenly Father. When I am troubled, do I do the same? Do you? Or do you automatically reach for the phone and call up another friend who's going through similar stresses of the military lifestyle? God created us to be in community with one another. He tells us in Galatians 6:2 to bear one another's burdens. Military wives do this exceptionally well! He wants us to encourage each other and pray for each other. The strong among us should hold up the weak. But next time you need to be uplifted, let the first call you make be to

God Himself. Take a moment alone with Him.

David said in Psalm 62:8 (NIV), "Trust in him at all times, O people; pour out your hearts to him, for God is our refuge." God desires to have the kind of relationship with us where we are quick to seek His counsel and direction in relation to the matters that concern us. In fact, His Word tells us that when we take our requests to God and leave our sources of anxiety at His feet, He will reward us with "the peace of God, which surpasses all comprehension" (Philippians 4:7).

I don't know about you, but it isn't very often that I hang up the phone after spewing my complaints to a friend that I can claim to have the peace of God. If anything, most of my well-meaning friends sympathize with me so much that I'm even more convinced that I am to be pitied. While it's always nice to be affirmed, God asks that we bring our burdens to Him and let Him take care of it. Jesus says, "Come to Me, all who are weary and heavy-laden, and I will give you rest" (Matthew 11:28).

Ask

When something is wrong, who do I call upon?
Am I allowing anything to replace my dependence on God?

Pray

Lord, Thank You for the people You've placed in my life to help me through challenging times—but let me never allow their presence to become more important to me than Your own. Help me to discipline myself to come to You first with my every need. In Jesus' Name, Amen.

by Sarah Ball

GOD OF ALL *Comfort*

Praise be to the God and Father of our Lord Jesus Christ,
the Father of compassion and the God of all comfort,
who comforts us in all our troubles,
so that we can comfort those in any trouble with
the comfort we ourselves have received from God.
2 CORINTHIANS 1:3–4 NIV

★ ★ ★

MY NEIGHBOR WAS DISTRAUGHT. "I missed my husband's phone call because I went to the grocery store. I've decided not to leave the house until he calls again."

Her husband was with an infantry battalion deployed to Iraq. Insurgents had captured several soldiers in his company the week before, and American forces were searching for them day and night. I knew that it might be days or weeks before her husband had the chance to call again. "Can I get you some groceries or something?" I asked her. "You can't just stay home for weeks without needing a few things."

"I don't eat much right now. I'm too worried. I can't sleep either. I just walk around the house and worry and hope that the phone rings. And then I hope it doesn't ring, because what if it's bad news? I told everyone in my husband's unit not to call me, because I can't handle hearing all the little updates. I only want the phone to ring if it is him." Her voice was almost brittle with fear. I prayed with her, brought her some groceries, and watched her continue her lonely vigil.

Fear, worry, and loneliness—they stalk all of us at one time or another. We deal with concerns for our husbands, our children, and our loved ones. The burdens are real. We cannot carry them alone.

The apostle Paul knew what it was like to carry burdens. He endured every kind of personal hardship and felt deep concern for the New Testament churches and believers. He wrote in 2 Corinthians 1:8 (NIV), "We do not want you to be uninformed, brothers, about the hardships we suffered in the province of Asia. We were under great pressure, far beyond our ability to endure, so that we despaired even of life."

Paul explained that God had allowed him to suffer so that Paul would not trust in his own strength, but rely on the comfort and deliverance of God the Father. In the end, Paul's suffering brought praise to God and allowed Paul to share comfort with others who were suffering.

I love the connection Paul makes between God's comfort to us and our comfort to others. We seek God's comfort and deliverance during our difficult times, but that isn't where the story ends. God wants us to receive His comfort and share it with others around us.

The day after I talked to my neighbor, I sat in our military women's Bible study and watched the comfort of God flow among the women. Women like my neighbor shared their fears about their husbands' safety, and we cried and prayed together for the safety of our missing soldiers. Unlike my neighbor, these women had chosen the comfort of God. They brought their burdens first to God, and then reached out for the hands of Christian women who could share the load.

Have I brought my fears and concerns
to the God of all comfort?
Who has God placed in my life right now
that needs the comfort of God?

Pray

Dear Lord, Thank You for being my compassionate heavenly Father. Please deliver me from the fears and worries that prey on my mind. Help me share Your comfort with others, so that You may receive even greater glory. In Jesus' Name, Amen.

by Vanessa Peters

LONELY *Christmas*

I bring you good news of great joy which will be for all the people; for today in the city of David there has been born for you a Savior, who is Christ the Lord.

LUKE 2:10–11

★ ★ ★

THOUGH I SAT IN A ROOM FULL OF PEOPLE, I'd never felt more alone. A big part of my heart was missing. My sweet husband was miles away in the Middle East. My children and I missed him terribly. Was this sacrifice really worth it? The selfish part of my heart said, "Let someone else fight. We need him here." On perhaps the most joyful day of the year, I sat at my parent's laughter-filled home, silently moping.

That's when my Dad handed me a card secretly sent from David. Through tear-filled eyes I read:

"To my love on Christmas,

"Oh, how I wish I were with you this blessed season—but God has other plans for us. And I trust Him. The Bible says, 'Blessed is he who trusts in the Lord' (Proverbs 16:20); He will bless us in due time. If not in this life, then in the glorious life to come which will far outshine all shadows of this age. . . . We are grounded in Him and therefore have hope—which outlasts earthly life and temporal deployments, sin, war, and even death. . . . I write to encourage you to put your hope and rest in Him—our Savior, who was once a child in a manger, a man of flesh, and also the risen and triumphant King over sin and death! He is my hope this season, our hope always, and I trust Him to comfort and be with you when I cannot. He is the reason why I love you . . . forever."

How God spoke right to my heart through my husband's letter! When I should have been rejoicing in the hope of Jesus, I was hoping David would walk through the door.

I wonder if Mary Livingstone ever felt the way I did on that lonely Christmas night? The wife of the great nineteenth-century English missionary, she and her husband, David, were apart more than half their married life. They once spent nearly four years separated, while he ministered to the needs of thousands of Africans unreached by the gospel or modern medicine. Mary raised six children nearly by herself. In 1862, shortly after the birth of their last child, Mary journeyed over land and sea to visit David for the last time. After three joyful months together, she died from malaria. David was devastated. And yet his perspective remained eternal. He did not cease his work; rather, as he mourned, he stated: "There is a Ruler above, and His Providence guides all things. He is our Friend, and has plenty of work for all His people to do . . . [which is] such a blessing and a privilege."[2]

Mary and I may have lived in different ages and married men of different vocations, but we shared one important thing: we both loved our husbands enough to let them fulfill God's calling.

That night, as I finished the letter, the most beautiful thing happened. God used the very one for whom my heart yearned to draw me back to Himself. It was Christmas, and indeed time to celebrate! "Joy to the world, the Lord has come!"

Ask

Am I content with what I have?
Do I place my trust in Christ alone for
my satisfaction and hope?

Pray

Lord, I often focus on myself and the pleasures of this life, when I should be looking to You and the hope of heaven. Turn my heart toward You when I lose perspective. In Jesus' Name, Amen.

by Lori Mumford

STRESS AND *Sin*

For we do not have a high priest who is unable to sympathize with our weaknesses, but we have one who has been tempted in every way, just as we are—yet was without sin. Let us then approach the throne of grace with confidence, so that we may receive mercy and find grace to help us in our time of need.
HEBREWS 4:15–16 NIV

★ ★ ★

ONCE DURING MY HUSBAND'S DEPLOYMENT, I had a frustrating, homeschooling day. My four-year-old needed much attention. I tried finishing housework so I could shop for my other daughter's upcoming birthday. Something was always interfering. I couldn't finish anything that day. The phone rang just as we were eating dinner, and before I answered, I thought, please, nobody ask anything else from me. They did, and then it happened: my youngest spilled her milk. As I watched it steadily pour onto the area rug, I closed my eyes and kept my composure while on the phone. When I hung up, I began ranting over my frustrations from the day. I could hear myself blabbing away. After I finished one subject, I went to another one. I couldn't shut up. After everything was wiped and rinsed, my youngest's eyes were still brimming with tears while the others looked hurt and sad. We all quietly stared at our plates of food, and I hated myself. I had sinned in my anger, and I needed forgiveness from my children and God.

When husbands are gone, there are additional pressures and

stress. With it comes more opportunities to sin. God hates sin no matter what excuse, but our Lord understands these heated times and actually sympathizes with us. By confessing sin and crying out to Him, our gracious, merciful Lord helps us when we seem unable to help ourselves. First John 1:9 says, "If we confess our sins, he is faithful and just and will forgive us our sins and purify us from all unrighteousness." His love is overwhelming.

When I regularly confess my sins and cry for help, I can better see the "way out" that He provides when I'm tempted again (1 Corinthians 10:13). Then, when life heats up, I'm more likely to take a breath before I blurt out careless words. When I start to vent, I hear in my head, "Stop!" This gives me hope of my Savior's work in me. Satan hates hope. He watches for another weak moment when I choose wrongly, then feel defeated and ashamed. But "He who began a good work in you will carry it on to completion until the day of Christ Jesus, (Philippians 1:6 NIV). He's not finished with us. Praise God that when we do falter, the throne of grace is always open. We can approach it with confidence and find grace and mercy to help us in our time of need. Thank you, Jesus!

Ask

What sinful behaviors arise when you're under more stress?
Do I confidently approach the throne of grace,
or does shame stop me?

Pray

Dear Lord, Thank You that You personally know what it means to be in this human body that's always tempted, and yet You were the only one who never sinned. Thank You for paying for my sins with Your sinless body. I haven't ever deserved it. Lord, forgive me of this sin of ________. Give me the grace to clearly see the way out that You provide so that my choices and my actions may be pleasing to You, my King. In Jesus' Name, Amen.

by Jocelyn Green

NO SEPARATION FROM *God's Love*

For I am convinced that neither death nor life,
nor angels nor principalities, nor things present,
nor things to come, nor powers, nor height nor depth,
nor any other created thing, will be able to separate us
from the love of God, which is in Christ Jesus our Lord.
ROMANS 8:38–39

★ ★ ★

DURING ONE DEPLOYMENT, I stood with the rest of the congregation one Sunday morning, singing the words that were flashed in giant letters on the screen up front. But on the inside, I was thinking about the distance (physical and emotional) that had been growing between me and my husband since he left. We were approaching nearly a month without any contact, and I felt sharply the disconnect between us.

As I jolted myself from my gloomy thoughts and listened to the words of my mouth, the irony of the situation hit me. Here I was pining away for a phone call or e-mail from my husband while I sang to God a chorus declaring that He was more than enough for me, that God satisfied me completely with His love.

God's love and saving grace really is all we need, and it is always available to us in abundant supply. Nothing can or will ever change that. It takes very little to separate military families. What a comfort to know that neither death nor life, nor height nor depth, neither land nor air nor sea, neither war nor rumors of war, neither time nor space can separate us from the love of God, which is in Christ Jesus. Praise the Lord!

During the times you feel overwhelmed with challenges you must face alone, consider Hebrews 13:5–6. "For He Himself has said, 'I will never desert you, nor will I ever forsake you,' so that we confidently say, 'The Lord is my helper, I will not be afraid. What will man do to me?'" Whether or not our husbands are with us, the Lord himself is our ever-present help in time of trouble.

The psalmist wrote, "Where can I go from Your Spirit? Or where can I flee from Your presence? If I ascend to heaven, You are there; if I make my bed in Sheol, behold, You are there. If I take the wings of the dawn, if I dwell in the remotest part of the sea, even there Your hand will lead me, and Your right hand will lay hold of me" (Psalm 139:7–10). There is no way—not even if we tried—that we as believers could ever be separated from the love of God!

Isaiah 54:10 says, "'For the mountains may be removed and the hills may shake, but My lovingkindness will not be removed from you, and My covenant of peace will not be shaken,' says the Lord who has compassion on you." May you be encouraged today with this promise of the unshakable, immovable, inseparable love of God, which is more than enough for all of your needs.

Ask

What need am I dwelling on that can be
met with God's love if I allow it?
How can I show the love of God to a lonely wife
I know this week?

Dear Lord, Thank You for being a God of love and compassion, for knowing my heart and bringing me comfort when I am lonely. Teach me to be fully satisfied in Your abundant love. Make my heart overflow with Your love so that I cannot help but bring that love to others who are hurting. In Jesus' Name, Amen.

by Marshéle Carter Waddell

Servant LEADERSHIP

Whoever wishes to become great among you shall be your servant . . . just as the Son of Man did not come to be served, but to serve, and to give his life as a ransom for many.
MATTHEW 20:26, 28

★ ★ ★

THE GREATEST SERVANT LEADER I've ever known is my husband. His heart beats to lead the men God has given to him—to train them, to prepare them for every circumstance, and to mentor them, passing on the faith, the wisdom, and the truths God has entrusted to him. I see Jesus continuing His earthly work through my husband, reaching the toughest, roughest soldiers in America with the love and truth of God, even on war fronts and in the dust storms and explosions of desert warfare.

My husband does not order his men to do anything he does not do. He is in training in the field, under the sea, above the earth, and freefalling through the clouds with them. The apostle Paul said, "I bear on my body the marks of Jesus" (Galatians 6:17 NIV). Paul was speaking of the marks left on his body as a result of his servant leadership. These marks were the proof in his physical body that he had followed Christ's call no matter what, serving as he led. My husband, too, bears in his body the marks of Jesus, the visible scars and the broken bones that have been the result of leading others by example, of leading others by serving them, even at great risk and cost to himself. He has poured himself out so that others could be freed and filled.

Isn't that what Jesus did for us? He led by example, requiring nothing more of His followers than what He was willing to do Himself, whether that meant humble service, emotional or physical suffering, or the ultimate sacrifice. He showed us how to do all of these things.

As military wives, we do not have troops under our command, but our realm of influence in our communities is no less significant. Women have always had an active role in sustaining the development of communities, safeguarding resources, educating youth, and ensuring continuity of social, cultural, and spiritual values. Think of the many lives you touch: your husband, your children and their teachers and friends, your extended families, other military families, civilian friends, and those in your church. It is just as important for us to be a servant leader within these realms as it is for those in military command.

Ask

Am I modeling servant leadership within my own family, and with other military wives?
What can I do to serve another family this week?
Prepare a meal? Offer babysitting? Run errands? Send a note?

Pray

Lord, I am not a warrior like my husband, yet I long to be a servant leader like him. I pray that I would bear the marks of Jesus on my body, too. The trail of a tear down my cheek as my friend shares her broken heart with me. Laugh lines around my eyes from rejoicing with those who rejoice. Calloused knees from kneeling by my bed and interceding for others. Dark circles under my tired eyes because I've awakened in the middle of the night unable to sleep because You were calling me to pray for someone. Strong arms because I've stirred stiff batters, lifted heavy boxes, and carried a child. Lord, I want to bear on my body the marks of Jesus, those visible markers that identify me as a follower of Christ. In Jesus' Name, Amen.

by Denise McColl

FINDING YOUR *Life*

And he who does not take his cross and follow after Me is not worthy of Me. He who has found his life will lose it, and he who has lost his life for My sake will find it.
MATTHEW 10:38–39

★ ★ ★

DURING MY MANY YEARS AS A NAVY WIFE, I've encountered some recurrent themes in my various circles of fellow military friends. Even in agreeing to this sort of "understood" sacrificial service, how easy it is to allow self-centered attitudes to creep in. We find ourselves questioning, "How can I fulfill my commitment to serve and hurt myself the least?"

In my quiet reading this morning I came across Matthew 10:38–39 (quoted above). It took quite a bit of dying to myself to "find my life" within the boundaries and framework of the military. What encouraged me to begin that dying process was the idea that "Whoever finds his life will lose it. . . . " The more I protected myself, agreed to serve or give "up to a point," finagled assignments, duty locations, perfect duty days, deployment requirements, the unhappier I became inside. Like a child throwing a tantrum to get her own way, I must have been a sight to behold. A false sense of camaraderie with other similarly "put-out" military wives began fueling my stance, my feelings, my seemingly justified reasons for trying to work and tweak situations so they would work best for me. I still remember the gnawing at my heart, the tugging at my conscience that grew each time I held fast to my "me-first" plan.

We must beware that well-meaning people may also encourage us to seek our own interests. Naval Reserves wife Leisa Gustafson's husband, Tim, was the first to be deployed from the Naval and Marine Corps Reserve Center Grand Rapids after September 11, 2001. One woman asked, "Can't you get out of this on hardship? You have five kids!" Tim's response was, "What would I teach my kids about following through with things even if you don't want to? I've been paid for years to train. When they ask me to do something, I've got to go." They knew it would be a challenge for the entire family, but they chose to take up their crosses and follow Christ, which includes obeying our earthly authorities.

Little by little, God exposed the ugliness of my old, selfish mind-set, and after a grave piercing of the heart, He began a remodeling process that wants to give and bend, instead of take and need. The more I saw the attitude in myself or my friends, the more my heart would break a little more, finally to be used for Him, instead of for me. The losing of my life (my will, desires, priorities, motives . . .) *for His sake* has been the greatest find! And I must admit, the rich life He has replaced for my search has been far better than anything I could have found on my own!

Ask

Am I consciously or subconsciously
trying to "tweak" this time in the military
so that everything falls into place
to fit my plans?
Am I frustrated and overly anxious in
trying to control that whole process?

God, Please help me to remember that as I lose my life for Your sake as I serve, that is where I will find it. Help me find peace in knowing that You will make good things of the things I just can't control. Help me to find the healthy balance of considering my family concerns, without needing to force my own way. Help me to trust you without tweaking! In Jesus' Name, Amen.

by Lasana Ritchie

FOUNDATION OF *Faith*

Therefore everyone who hears these words of mine and puts them into practice is like a wise man who built his house on the rock. The rain came down, the streams rose, and the winds blew and beat against that house; yet it did not fall, because it had its foundation on the rock. But everyone who hears these words of mine and does not put them into practice is like a foolish man who built his house on sand. The rain came down, the streams rose and the winds blew and beat against that house, and it fell with a great crash.

MATTHEW 7:24–27 NIV

★ ★ ★

I'VE HEARD THE SAYING IN THE NAVY, "It's not enough to be flexible, one has to be fluid." Too true! On two occasions, our friends received orders, packed up the house, and received a mid-move call with revised orders to return to the previous station! I was personally challenged on our return from England, when my husband was asked to accept revised orders requiring him to deploy to war six months earlier than planned. He returned home for four months, and was again called to the same war. He then stayed home for nearly a year and was called to return again. With four children, three of whom are ADHD or ADD, I was tired. It was good not to be functioning on my own power.

My position has always been one of trust. I know I cannot

protect my husband even on the streets of my hometown from accident, injury, or death, let alone on the battlefield. However, God is powerful enough to protect him anywhere. That was fine head knowledge, but when I actually saw my husband on the news in his bulletproof/gas prevention attire, talking about a service done for five Marines who were killed in the line of duty, it became a matter of survival to trust God. In times like these, my foundation and heart must be solid, or the "winds of the sea" will carry me further off course than I might imagine.

The Tower of Pisa's construction was flawed from the beginning because of its weak foundation. They attempted to fix the lean without addressing the cause by building higher floors with one side higher than the other. The solution was creative but flawed. The Tower appeared straight when seen from a distance, but it still leaned.

In our own lives, our only hope of standing straight and tall through every storm is our foundation of faith. Faith allows us to rise above our circumstances. If our faith is strong, we will not fall when the winds and waves of our trials come crashing in around us. Faith like this—faith strong enough to build a military life upon!—is never based on circumstances or on our feelings. It is based on God's character and rooted in the Word of God. Notice from Jesus' parable (quoted above) that the man who built his foundation on the rock was not immune to storms, but he could withstand them because of his right foundation.

Ask

What is my foundation?
Am I more anchored in God's character
or in my emotional reactions to circumstances?

Dear Lord, Search me for ways that keep me from fully embracing You and Your plans. I surrender all to You. Build beneath me Your firm foundation. May your truth penetrate to my spirit and give me peace. I commit to You all the unknowns of my life on the seas of this life, and may I find my sufficiency in You whether in storm or calm. In Jesus' Name, Amen.

Section Five

TOTAL SURRENDER:

Giving Up Our Attempts to Be in Control

"For I know the plans I have for you," declares the Lord,
"plans for welfare and not for calamity
to give you a future and a hope."

JEREMIAH 29:11

by Jocelyn Green

WHEN SURRENDER MEANS *Victory*

"For I know the plans that I have for you," declares the Lord, "plans for welfare and not for calamity to give you a future and a hope."
JEREMIAH 29:11

★ ★ ★

FROM THE FIRST WEEK of her new husband's deployment to Iraq until he came home, Melissa Gardner would cry every Sunday in church, like clockwork. "About halfway through the deployment I began to realize I wasn't crying because I missed Mike or because I was sad," she says. "I would sit in church and feel so unbelievably helpless and small compared to God's capacity to take care of us. I cried during worship because I felt just so thankful for His magnitude, and because it was such a relief to submit to His control. Resting in the Lord's strength, not my own, was an overwhelming comfort."

Melissa learned that her emotional and spiritual survival was inexorably linked to her belief that God was in control all over the world, from her husband's base in Falljuah, Iraq, to her home in Washington, D.C. Only when she surrendered to His plan and provision was she released from the grip of fear.

The Bible is full of heroes of the faith who were surrendered to God's plan before they were used of Him. When the Lord told Abram to leave his country with virtually no explanation, Abram left (Genesis 12:4). When Mary learned that she was suddenly carrying the Messiah in her womb, she responded with, "Behold, the bondslave of the Lord; may it be done to me according to your word" (Luke 1:38).

May we be so surrendered to God's plan for us that when facing adversity, we can echo Job's sentiments when he said: "The Lord gave and the Lord has taken away. Blessed be the name of the Lord, . . . Shall we indeed accept good from God and not accept adversity?" (Job 1:21, 2:10).

Though he was "grieved to the point of death," Jesus surrendered to God's plan for his impending crucifixion at Gethsemane (Matthew 26:39, 42).

Nancy Leigh DeMoss says that God asks us to sign a blank contract for our life and let Him fill in all the details afterward:

> "Why? Because I am God; because I have bought you; because I am trustworthy; because you know how much I love you; because you live for My glory and not your own independent, self-promoting pleasure."
>
> [When signing that blank paper,] we cannot lose, because He is a God who can be completely trusted. If we will let Him, God will fill in the details of our lives with His incomparable wisdom and sovereign plan, written in the indelible ink of His covenant faithfulness and love.[1]

When we surrender to Christ, we are surrendering not to an enemy, as in war, but to our greatest advocate! By relinquishing our control to One much more powerful and wise than ourselves, we can trust that not only will our basic needs be met, but we will be spiritually nourished as well. For us, to surrender to Christ is resounding victory for God's glory.

Ask

Am I holding back from surrendering
any areas of my life to God?
What could I gain if I were to give to Christ my fears,
anxiety, and desire to control?

Pray

Lord, Increase my faith and give me the discipline and courage so that I might surrender my life, my hopes, and my dreams to You daily. Help me to desire Your glory more than my own comfort and convenience. Show me what it means to be submitted to You. In Jesus' Name, Amen.

by Lasana Ritchie

Resistance

In all things God works for the good of those who love him, and who have been called according to his purpose.
ROMANS 8:28

★ ★ ★

HAVE YOU EVER HAD ORDERS CHANGED when you were adjusted? What do we do when all we do doesn't fit the plan we had in our heads?

"Resistance" sometimes gets a bad rap. It is often associated with (1) opposition to somebody or something, (2) refusal to accept or comply with something, (3) the ability to remain unaltered by the damaging effect of something, and (4) the ability to refrain from something in spite of being tempted. These are all negative qualities. Can there be anything positive about resistance? I think so.

An airplane leaves the ground only against the wind. Without this resistance it could never gain the height to lift it into the air and soar over the clouds. Without a clutch, our standard-shift cars would be motoring around in first gear all day—imagine how much shopping you couldn't get done in first gear! Want to sharpen your pencil? You push your pencil into sharpening mechanisms of various sorts and the blades cut away the unwanted wood to reveal the lead, making a sharp point.

Now let's take this illustration and apply it to our lives. Romans 8:28 says that God works "in all things." The enemy has a plan for our lives too—ruin and eternal destruction. But

God can work even with the bad things that happen to good people, turning to good what the enemy meant for evil.

Here's a thought my father gave me long ago that still holds me steadfast in uncertain times: "God cares what happens in us more than what happens to us." That doesn't mean He doesn't care what happens to us—on the contrary, He uses all things to work together for our inner good. He's big enough to use anything; who am I to doubt Him by what He brings my way?

We hold on to the idea of what we might think is best for us—the right duty station, the right car, the right house, the right job, the image of what our children should do in life—but having our hands open to let go willingly in surrender allows God the authority in our lives. After all, He has eternity in mind, not just the present, and He is shaping us in His image.

Ask

Am I allowing God to carve away unnecessary wood shavings,
to shift my gears, and blow in my face to raise me
to the level of the clouds and see eternity?
Am I too full of the present to let go and trust Him?
Am I truly surrendered in all areas of my life?

Pray

Lord, Take my heart and loosen the ties that keep me bound to only a temporal view of my life. Give me Your perspective and Your view of my circumstances. Help me with the changes that come to me, upsetting my plans and expectations. Help me rest in You in surrender, knowing You are my hiding place and know the paths You want my heart to walk, and let me hold Your hand—be my Guide. In Jesus' Name, Amen.

by Jill Hart

DEPENDING ON *Him*

My salvation and my honor depend on God;
he is my mighty rock, my refuge.
PSALM 62:7 NIV

★ ★ ★

I LEARNED SOON AFTER MARRYING AN AIRMAN that any time I called to make an appointment somewhere on base, I'd be asked if I was a "dependent." This struck a nerve with me. I hated that term—dependent. It made me think of being weak, useless. Didn't they know how "independent" I was?!

However, a year and a half into our marriage I began having fevers every day. They would come and go each day, but left me worn out. As the months wore on, I saw several doctors at the base hospital and went through rounds and rounds of tests. I struggled to even get out of bed each morning, let alone care for our eight-month-old daughter, Katy.

During this time, my husband and family stepped up—taking leave, watching Katy, and shuttling me to and fro. I began to see how truly dependent I was. Being sick, I was forced to rely on my family. God began to show me that allowing myself to accept the help of others was not a sign of weakness, but of wisdom. Although I was miserable being sick, I felt loved and sheltered in both the love of God and my family. I became very thankful to be someone's "dependent."

The same thing is true in our spiritual lives. When we try to rely on ourselves and work our way into God's favor we fail every time. But when we allow ourselves to be dependent on Him, to rest in His love for us, it's then that we can extend that love to others.

The story of Jonah is a great example of someone who tries to go his own way, only to find that dependence on the Lord is the only thing that can save him. When Jonah boards a ship headed in the opposite direction of where God has asked him to go, he finds himself the cause of a terrible storm that threatens the life of everyone on board. After trying to steady the ship on their own, the sailors decide to listen to Jonah and throw him overboard. God sends a big fish to swallow Jonah and keeps him there three days until Jonah is ready to do what God has asked of him.

Jonah thought he knew what was best for himself and for his fellow countrymen. God goes to great lengths to get Jonah's full attention. When Jonah finally admits his dependence on God for his very life and submits to Him, the entire great city of Nineveh repents and returns to following the Lord.

When we, like Jonah, admit that we are dependent on the Lord—that we are God's "dependents"—who knows what wonderful things He might accomplish through us?

Ask

Am I working to earn God's favor
or relying on His gift of salvation?
Do I tend to think I know what's best for me
and for those around me?
Am I so concerned with being "independent" that
I've lost sight of what dependence on God truly means?

Dear Lord, It can be hard to stop relying on myself and to simply rest in Your love. Help me to accept Your grace and kindness and to extend that love to others. The story of your faithfulness to Jonah despite his arrogance and disobedience gives me hope that You can use even a sinner like me. Thank You for Your forgiveness and love. In Jesus' Name, Amen.

by Lori Mumford

THE PERFECT *Place*

Come now, you who say, "Today or tomorrow we will go to such and such a city, and spend a year there and engage in business and make a profit." Yet you do not know what your life will be like tomorrow. You are just a vapor that appears for a little while and then vanishes away. Instead, you ought to say, "If the Lord wills, we will live and also do this or that."

JAMES 4:13–16 NIV

★ ★ ★

MY HUSBAND AND I had many conversations about the perfect place to transfer next. They'd go something like this: *After this tour, we could go to that place, then transfer to this place for a few years where we could moonlight for some extra money. The last tour, we could go there where we could retire.*

We poured over the possibilities to secure the future we wanted. One day, I read James 4:13–16, and I was convicted we were boasting about tomorrow. I showed the verse to my husband, and we were struck by how plain it was in the Bible and how so plainly wrong we were.

We can easily think the future is in our control if we plan right. My husband and I stressed about getting shore stations for the benefit of our young family. Not only did he get a boat, but he was gone for over half the first year. Without that experience, I never would have seen such a display of God's awesome power, grace, and work in our lives. This forced me to cry out to Him, and He met our needs.

Satan cloaks selfish desires. He convinces us that something or somewhere can make us happy, because after all, God wants us happy, right? He tempts us to believe that a selfish desire is also God's desire for us. We think we know what we want. However, our will can never fulfill us like His will.

If I panic or become angry about the next transfer, then I know I've put my trust in my own desires and plans. I must trust His plans. I'm still selfish, and sometimes I have to ask Him for the "desire" to desire His will. In Psalm 37:4, it says, "Delight yourself in the Lord and He will give you the desires of your heart." Does that mean we get what we want as a rule? No! It means trusting Him first and desiring His will over ours. He changes our selfish desires when we say, "Your will be done" (Matthew 6:10).

We still look at potential places. After much prayer, we write down our choice number one, two, three, etc., on the "dream sheet," but we realize they are only places we think are good for us. God may have better plans, even if it's hard to see initially. We're reminded that we truly have no idea what's best for us, but He does. Isaiah 48:17 (NIV) says, "This is what the Lord says, your Redeemer, the Holy One of Israel: I am the Lord your God, who teaches you what is best for you, who directs you in the way you should go." With that, I say, "Teach and direct me!"

Ask

Do I make plans and boast about tomorrow?
Whose plans will never fail me?

Pray

Dear Lord, Help me want Your desire for me. Help me trust where You'll take us, because even when Your will doesn't seem easy, Lord, You know what is best for me. Thank You for Your love and care for me. In Jesus' Name, Amen.

by Rebekah Benimoff with Jocelyn Green

Trust

Trust in the Lord with all your heart, and lean not on your own understanding. Acknowledge Him in all your ways, and He shall direct your paths.

PROVERBS 3:5–6 NKJV

★ ★ ★

A FEW MONTHS after my (Rebekah's) husband returned from Iraq, he began having emotional difficulties. About this time, our family moved across the country to a new duty station. I was separated from my support system at a time I needed them most. My chaplain husband was angry with God, life, everything. He vacillated between extremes—anger, sorrow, depression, bitterness, despair. I was overwhelmed by the pendulum-like swings of his behavior. At times I felt that there was no trace of the man I married.

I was grieving. Grieving the loss of the husband I knew, and grieving the loss of "the dream" of what our family life would be like. I was also grieving the relationships with friends I had left behind.

During this period, I discovered that some of my trust had been misguided. I had begun to trust in God's actions rather than God's character. There is a great difference between asking "What am I trusting God for?" rather than "Who am I trusting?" My focus became skewed, and I started to look for God to DO SOMETHING, instead of waiting in Him.

Lamentations 3:25–26 (NIV) says, "The Lord is good to

those whose hope is in him, to the one who seeks him; it is good to wait quietly for the salvation of the Lord."

Sometimes the storms of life shift our focus from our original purpose, which is to know God intimately. We must hold to the truth that God is a loving God, even when circumstances force us beyond where we would have chosen to follow.

Consider the plight of Naomi and Ruth. When a famine hits Bethlehem, Naomi's family moves to Moab, where her husband dies. Her two sons marry two Moabites, Ruth and Orpah, but after ten years of infertility for both couples, the men die. These women are left to fend for themselves in an ancient culture in which women are valued and cared for according to their male connections.

Yet it is at this point that Ruth makes the radical decision to follow Naomi—and her God. "Your people will be my people, and your God, my God" (Ruth 1:16). Clearly, her decision to follow Yahweh instead of her old Moabite gods was not based on the good fortune of her circumstances, but on who she had learned Yahweh to be.

Carolyn Custis James writes, "We live in the realm of faith, and that means trusting God for who he is and not because things equal out or we have satisfying answers to our questions. Faith may want answers, but somehow it is able to survive without them."[2]

When my trust wavers, it is always because I have lost sight of who God is. Throughout your own storms of life, let your anchor be God's character.

Ask

What do you believe about God's character
that affects how you relate to Him when
life's circumstances are troubling?

Pray

Lord, First John 4:8 reminds me that Your very nature is love. When my trust in You is shaken, remind me of Your character. As I journey through the difficult places in this life, teach me to draw near to You and be covered in Your great love for me. El-shaddai, You are sufficient for the needs of Your people. Give me courage and hope as I choose to trust You with all my heart. In Jesus' Name, Amen.

by Sarah Ball

So then, just as you received Christ Jesus as Lord, continue to live in him, rooted and built up in him, strengthened in the faith as you were taught, and overflowing with thankfulness.
COLOSSIANS 2:6–7 NIV

★ ★ ★

I GREW UP IN TYPHOON TERRITORY. Each rainy season brought giant storms sweeping across our island home. We'd board over the windows, stock up on canned food, and wait out the onslaught of water and wind. Occasionally a really big typhoon caused catastrophic damage, but most of the typhoons were just "banana typhoons"—the only casualties they caused were uprooted banana trees.

Banana trees (which are actually classified as large herbs, not trees) have amazingly small root systems relative to their top growth. A large group of banana trees can topple and leave only a small hole in the ground. By contrast, a tropical banyan tree can leave a root crater large enough to hold several teens. In fifteen years, I saw thousands of uprooted banana trees, but only two banyan trees. The difference was all in the roots.

I no longer live in the typhoon-battered tropics, but I have realized that life contains many storms that can't be forecast by weather radar. Deployments, financial need, illness, loneliness, and loss blow through our lives, testing the spiritual roots by which we are grounded.

Psalm 1 describes two different types of lives and the roots that hold them. "Blessed is the man who does not walk in the counsel of the wicked or stand in the way of sinners or sit in the seat of mockers. But his delight is in the law of the Lord, and on his law he meditates day and night. He is like a tree planted by streams of water, which yields its fruit in season and whose leaf does not wither. Whatever he does prospers. Not so the wicked! They are like chaff that the wind blows away" (verses 1–4 NIV).

The first man makes a clear choice to delight in the law of the Lord, so his spiritual roots are deep, he is refreshed by life-giving water, and he produces spiritual fruit without withering. The second man rejects God's law and is left rootless and vulnerable to life's hardships.

We encounter both types of people in the context of military life. I have watched women endure months of physical pain, separation from their husbands, grief, and loss. Those who were rooted in God's Word remained fully anchored, and their hope and dignity were beautiful fruit in the middle of suffering. Women who relied on their own strength and understanding instead of a relationship with God were quickly shown to be rootless, and their emotional need was painful to see.

Paul's instructions to the Colossians tell us how to prepare for the storms that are inevitable in our lives. We have received Christ as Lord, but we need to continue to be rooted and built up in Him, strengthening our faith through God's Word. The daily process of deepening our spiritual roots will keep us prepared for whatever size storm may come.

Ask

What storms are blowing in my life right now?
Have I rooted myself firmly in God's Word
to hold me steady during difficult times?

Dear Lord, Thank You for being the God of the universe, greater than any storm that threatens my life. I want to anchor myself in You, so that I can stand firm in every circumstance. Please strengthen my faith as I delight and meditate in Your Word and walk daily with You. In Jesus' Name, Amen.

by Sara Horn

TRUSTING GOD IN THE *Unknown*

He will have no fear of bad news;
his heart is steadfast, trusting in the Lord.
PSALM 112:7 NIV

★ ★ ★

IT WAS 11:30 AT NIGHT when my cell phone's ring woke me up. Cliff's Navy Reserve unit had been in Iraq for a month, and life for both of us finally seemed more routine. He called and e-mailed a couple of times a week. I felt good—things were more predictable.

Then Cliff mentioned that he and some of his friends were getting dinner at Taco Bell.

My heart stopped. This was the code word we agreed to use if Cliff ever had to leave for a mission. The base was the only place he'd worked since arriving, and I'd convinced myself he would stay there for the entire deployment. But I was wrong. He was going outside the wire, and I had no idea what was next.

Tears fell down my cheeks.

The confidence I felt just a moment before was completely gone. My husband was on the other side of the world, heading into parts unknown, facing real dangers, and there was nothing I could do. I felt helpless and lost.

Before he hung up, we prayed together. When it was my turn to pray, trying to keep the emotion out of my voice, I asked God to watch over Cliff, to protect him until he came home. I asked, but in my heart I was telling God in no uncertain terms that He would protect my husband and He would bring him home safe. Or else!

After we said we loved each other and Cliff promised to call as soon as he could, I put the phone down, leaned back on my pillow, and cried.

That's when I sensed God ask me a very important question.

Am I in control?

Feeling very convicted, I said yes.

And don't you think I am with your husband in Iraq just as I'm with you right now?

Yes.

Then trust Me. And remember that even if you don't know what will happen tomorrow, I do.

We don't know what tomorrow will bring. Whether we face it in a deployment or a performance review or a health scare or financial crisis, we don't know what will happen. But God does. Jeremiah reminds us, "For I know the plans I have for you," declares the Lord, "plans to prosper you and not to harm you, plans to give you hope and a future" (Jeremiah 29:11 NIV).

Grace Fox reminds us of four basic truths we can hold on to when we're facing the unknown:

1. God remains steadfast amid life's uncertainties.
2. God cares about the details of our lives.
3. God brings good from every trial.
4. God always keeps His promises.[3]

We don't know about tomorrow. But we do know God is faithful. Remember His faithfulness when the shadows of uncertainty creep in. Trust He is there.

Ask

What unknowns in life am I afraid of right now?
Where have I seen God's faithfulness in the past?
Where have I seen His faithfulness today?

Pray

Lord, Thank you that when nothing else is sure in life, Your love for me never changes. Help me remember that when I worry about tomorrow, You already know what's to come, and You will be there with me no matter what. Give me peace today in the knowledge that You are the only thing certain in life, and the only certainty I need. In Jesus' Name, Amen.

by Sarah Ball

SLOW *Down*

Be still, and know that I am God.
PSALM 46:10

★ ★ ★

IF YOU WERE TO ATTACH A SPEEDOMETER to your day, what would your average speed be? I think my speed would hover between "barely legal" and "out of control" on some days. I've got carpools, sporting events, commissary stops, Bible studies, Family Readiness Group meetings, doctor's appointments, and To Do lists that are never done. Sometimes just looking at my calendar makes me feel tired!

There are many reasons we end up in such a hurry—we have a hard time saying no to people, we want our kids to have as many opportunities as possible, we desire to help our friends and neighbors. We try to keep up with all the "super moms" around us, but our husbands' duties often leave us in the role of "single mom." It's as if we think that our value is measured by the things that we do. After all, a busy person must be an important person, right?

I'm thankful that God does not measure our worth by the length of our list of accomplishments. He created us for friendship with Himself, but our busy lives are costing us the chance to have a deep friendship with Him.

John Ortberg doesn't pull any punches when talking about our hurried lives. "Hurry is the great enemy of spiritual life in our day. Hurry can destroy our souls. Hurry can keep us from living well. . . . Again and again, as we pursue spiritual life, we must do battle with hurry. For many of us the great danger is not that we will renounce our faith. It is that we will become so distracted and rushed and preoccupied that we will settle for a mediocre version of it. We will just skim our lives instead of actually living them."[4]

That last sentence really caught my attention. I don't want to skim my life. I want to live it fully, enjoying my family, my friendship with God, and all the wonderful little blessings God brings my way.

God showed me that I needed to slow myself down and build into my life a greater margin—time not filled with activity, a sort of buffer zone before I reach the point of exhaustion.

I prayed about my own need for a margin, and God led me to give up one of my weekly commitments. That opened a free day in my week, which became my margin for the rest of the week. It is the day that I have time to respond to anything that God may be laying on my heart— more time with my kids, a neighbor in need of encouragement, or my own need to be still and listen to God.

How much margin do you have in your life right now? Margin in your life may not look the same as in mine, but we all need some space between ourselves and our limits. When we stop the hurry and build in some margin, we can live as fully and deeply as God intends.

Ask

Is my busy pace limiting my relationship with God and others?
In what areas might God want me to slow down
and create more space for Him?

Pray

Dear Lord, I desire to live my life fully and deeply with You. Show me how to set a pace that honors You, values my family, and provides the margin that I need. In Jesus' Name, Amen.

by Sara Horn

Superwoman OR SUPER STRESSED?

As Jesus and his disciples were on their way, he came to a village where a woman named Martha opened her home to him. She had a sister called Mary, who sat at the Lord's feet listening to what he said. But Martha was distracted by all the preparations that had to be made. She came to him and asked, "Lord, don't you care that my sister has left me to do the work by myself? Tell her to help me!" "Martha, Martha," the Lord answered, "you are worried and upset about many things, but only one thing is needed. Mary has chosen what is better, and it will not be taken away from her."

LUKE 10:38–41NIV

★ ★ ★

POOR MARTHA. We have made her the poster child for over-achievers everywhere. She is the shameless example we all point to when we talk about wrong priorities, the superwoman we don't want to emulate, the Bible character we all say we don't want to be. Yet, if we were honest, most of us are exactly like her.

As the wife of a Navy reservist, I felt the pressures of being a civilian superwoman long before I felt the need to be a super military wife. So it was a natural progression that when my husband was activated for his first deployment, I knew I would have to be super-organized, super-motivated, and super-together. After all, the active military wives I knew seemed on top of things, so ready for whatever happened.

No matter what kind of organizational skills God has given you, there will always be more you feel like you should be doing. It isn't enough to manage the home, family, church activities, children's activities, and all of the other things we volunteer to take on; and if we're already managing all that, we think we should be doing it a lot better. Eventually, though, our superwoman selves hit the wall, and we struggle to keep from losing our capes completely.

Whether you're PCSing to a new town, getting ready to be a single mom for another year's deployment, or dealing with other life changes that bring new and sometimes overwhelming responsibilities, it is easy to forget that our "do" is not as important as our "be."

God wants our focus to rest on Him. But if every hour of the day is filled to the second with meetings and chores and multiple pages of to-do lists, when can we simply sit and listen, like Mary, for what He has to say?

Joanna Weaver talks about the importance of unloading a too-busy life. She gives three steps to follow:

1. Make a list of all of the activities you and your family do.
2. Pray over that list and prioritize it, assigning each a number from one to four.
3. Eliminate all the fours.[5]

By dumping some of the things you do that aren't really as important as you thought, you will free up time to focus on the One who can make all of your burdens light.

"Come to Me all you who labor and are heavy-laden and I will give you rest" (Matthew 11:28).

Ask

What am I doing today that is really important?
What are things I'm doing that I can cut out?

Lord, Thank you for always being the One I can turn to and for reminding me that I don't have to do it all alone. Give me wisdom to choose what is truly important and what isn't. In Jesus' Name, Amen.

by Jocelyn Green

IS GOD *Trustworthy?*

"For my thoughts are not your thoughts,
nor are your ways My ways," declares the Lord.
ISAIAH 55:8

★ ★ ★

ON SEPTEMBER 11, 2001, Navy wife Deshua Joyce tried to think positively when she heard the news that a plane had crashed into the Pentagon, where her husband worked. She thought, *What are the chances that his office was hit?* Still, her heart was heavy with concern for her husband, Tom, and all others at the Pentagon.

In fact, the plane crashed through the building directly under his floor, completely destroying his office. Miraculously, Tom escaped unscathed and was able to notify Deshua of his safety within an hour. Deshua's gratitude for Tom's escape was tempered with grief for those who did not. "I remember thinking at the end of the day, 'People's lives are changed forever,'" she said. "I was devastated for the loved ones of those who never made it out."

When Tom reunited with his family after the attack, he read Psalm 91 with them, which seemed to be written just for him. His oldest son asked, "What are you going to do with the rest of your life that God spared today?" After Tom retired from the military, he became a pastor.

While many lives that could have been lost on that fateful day were preserved, we know the rest of the story. We remember the news broadcasts and the newspaper headlines. If you walked through Ground Zero, you saw all the photos pinned up by friends and family. Ready or not, about 2,973 souls were sent to eternity that day.

On that day, and every day, how does God choose which lives to safeguard and which to call into the next life? I don't know the answer. I'm sure no one does. The larger question is this: Is God trustworthy? Can we trust Him to be in control of every moment in every part of the globe? If we say yes, we admit that He presides over tragedy. If we say we cannot trust Him in all things, we cannot trust Him at all. If He is not all-powerful, He is not God.

God refers to himself as "Sovereign Lord" 303 times in the Bible.[6] Jerry Bridges notes in *Trusting God*: "God's sovereignty is . . . exercised in infinite wisdom, far beyond our ability to comprehend. God's plan and His ways of working out His plan are frequently beyond our ability to fathom and understand. We must learn to trust when we don't understand."[7]

When we can't figure out God's plan for our lives or for those around us, we must rest in His sovereignty instead.

Ask

Does my belief in God's sovereignty rely on my circumstances or on what the Bible tells me of God's character?

Pray

Lord, When I am tempted to believe that You are only a good God if Your plan matches up with mine, remind me that Your thoughts, Your ways, are higher than mine. When I don't understand what You are doing, help me dwell instead on who You are. Help me to lean not on my own understanding but to trust You with all my heart (Proverbs 3:5–6). In Jesus' Name, Amen.

by Sheryl Shearer

GOD IS MY *Pilot*

Who of you by worrying can add a single hour to your life?
Since you cannot do this very little thing,
why do you worry about the rest?
LUKE 12:25–26 NIV

★ ★ ★

WHAT BEGAN AS A ROUTINE 37-week checkup with my third pregnancy turned into a free fall of fear and anxiety. Doctors discovered that the baby was wrapped in the umbilical cord and I would need to be induced immediately.

Having moved to this base only six months earlier and with my husband out to sea, I panicked. Worry consumed me: Who should I call? Who *can* I call? How am I going to give birth to this baby *by myself*? Will the baby be all right? Who will watch my kids? Where is my car parked, and will it be towed? My bag is not packed, and we have not purchased an infant car seat yet!

Little by little, God showed His faithfulness, beginning with wheeling me into the birthing room named after my husband's ship, the USS *Sacramento*. I thought the nursing staff did this purposefully, but this just *happened* to be the only room available. A conversation with the captain's wife became a divinely orchestrated transition between the initial shock-and-awe to a peaceful assurance to face my predicament. God further revealed His care for me by meeting all of my needs through the incredible medical staff, a female chaplain, my pastor's wife, and a military couple from our church. The loving actions of these people collectively served as God's reminder that He was with me.

Circumstances and sources—large and small—including family, finances, health, and simple daily concerns trigger worry. Medical studies reveal a connection between worry and early death. The psychological effects of worry cause irritability, moodiness, and an inability to make decisions. One thing is certain: we will encounter obstacles and challenges. The key is not allowing worry to consume and destroy us. Releasing our fear of the unknown to God is a starting point. With the psalmist, we can say, "When I am afraid, I will put my trust in you" (Psalm 56:3).

In his book *Ruthless Trust,* Brennan Manning offers some perspective on trusting God, something he calls "radical dependence." He says, "Like faith and hope, trust cannot be self-generated. I cannot simply *will* myself to trust. What outrageous irony: the one thing that I am responsible for throughout my life I cannot generate. The one thing I *need* to do I *cannot* do. . . . Why waste time beating myself up for something I cannot affect? What *does* lie within my power is paying attention to the faithfulness of Jesus. That's what I am asked to do: pay attention to Jesus throughout my journey, remember his kindnesses (Psalm 103:2)."[8] When we relinquish control to God, we experience a shift in focus from the problem to God's virtue and faithfulness.

Another by-product of surrendering control to God is divine peace. Detachment from the overwhelming urge to control our situation, which we ultimately cannot do, allows us to hear God's voice in our circumstance and, thus, His plan for us. Yielding to God makes way for His unsurpassable peace, and turns the storm raging in our hearts into a quiet calm.

Do I find myself worrying instead of trusting God
when faced with life's difficulties?
What keeps me from releasing my fears to God?

Pray

"God, give us grace to accept with serenity the things that cannot be changed, courage to change the things which should be changed, and the wisdom to distinguish the one from the other. In Jesus' Name, Amen."
—Reinhold Niebuhr[9]

Section Six

THE PRICE OF DUTY:

Overcoming the Trials Inherent in Serving

After you have suffered for a little while,
the God of all grace, who called you to His eternal glory
in Christ, will Himself perfect, confirm,
strengthen and establish you.

1 PETER 5:10

by Marshéle Carter Waddell

WEARY *Hearts*

Wait on the Lord; be of good courage, and He shall strengthen your heart; Wait, I say, on the Lord!
PSALM 27:14 NKVJ

★ ★ ★

MY MARRIAGE is brain-dead. There are no signs of life. Only the slow, monotonous drip of an intravenous routine. Surely this is not the God-design for my marriage.

I watch my marriage melt like a snowman, temperatures rising beyond what it is able to endure. Slipping away is everything I desired in life: a romantic, growing marriage. A home where children feel safe and secure. Children who walk in the Truth. A place in community. A familiar land. Though I have worked faithfully to these ends, today in my weariness, I cannot see any of this.

Hopelessness and the temptation to quit nip at my heels today—but deep down, I don't want this marriage to fail. So I stay and I walk through my house like I walk though my days . . . alive only because of the drip of the IV of daily time spent with my Lord. I mourn the loss of myself. I fear that the storms have finally swept me away.

Perhaps like me, you can identify with David when he says, "O my God, I cry by day, but You do not answer; and by night I have no rest" (Psalm 22:2). Just a few chapters later, he says, "Weeping may last for the night, but a shout of joy comes in the morning" (Psalm 30:5). Though we may feel stuck in the night David speaks of, we must choose to believe that morning will come and the Lord will revive our hearts.

One of my favorite names for the Holy Spirit is the Comforter (John 14:26 KJV). In other translations of the Bible, the Holy Spirit is called the Helper. Jesus said, "I will ask the Father, and He will give you another Helper, that He may be with you forever; that is the Spirit of truth" (John 14:16–17). When we turn to the Holy Spirit for help and comfort, He will not only give us aid, but He will give us a richer portion of His presence than we have ever had before. When we mourn, we will be blessed with comfort from the Comforter Himself (Matthew 5:4).

Ask

When I am weary, where do I seek solace? Other people? Food? The Lord? Try memorizing God's promises for you: Isaiah 40:28–31 and 1 Peter 5:10 are good places to start.

Pray

Father of compassion and God of all comfort, You tell me to put my hope in You. You say that nothing is impossible with God. Lord, I need Your power. I can say along with Paul that I know whom I have believed . . . YOU! I am convinced that You are able to guard what I have entrusted to You for that day. I ask You to guard my marriage and my love and devotion for the man You gave to me. Thank You for my husband. Bless and protect him today. Make me the wife You intended me to be for him today. In Jesus' Name, Amen.

by Sheryl Shearer

THE COMPANIONSHIP OF *Loneliness*

"Surely I am with you always."
MATTHEW 28:20 NIV

★ ★ ★

MILITARY FAMILIES AND MOVING are synonymous. They go together like peanut butter and jelly. Our families use a separate address book just for us! Picking up our lives every two to three years (on the average) and settling in a new place can be both exciting and unsettling. I value meeting new people, living in new places, and gaining exposure to different cultures. Yet, on the flip side are serious challenges, one of which is loneliness.

Loneliness hitches a ride as a constant, albeit unwanted, companion. I may have experienced the treasures of new people and places, but my nonmilitary family and friends have remained in the same places with the same people growing the same relationships. They have a continuity that I begin to envy: they experience life together.

How can I combat loneliness in this mobile lifestyle?

The permanence of my relationship with the Lord anchors me and provides continual companionship. I stay close to Jesus through prayer, meditation, reading Scripture, and serving. Regardless of my change of address, I know that God walks with me through the seasons and changes of life.

While this divine relationship is invaluable and irreplaceable,

God created humans as social creatures, craving and desiring companionship with one another. We expect this with our family, but experiencing that same unconditional care and comradeship with others not linked to us by blood creates a deep bond. This is especially evident within our military and faith communities. Some of my most cherished memories are when strangers, acquaintances, and new friends express love.

After a recent move, I became severely ill during the early stages of my fourth pregnancy. When the word got out on the base about my condition, new friends and neighbors brought dinners, helped watch our kids, and brought me home from the hospital when my husband, who is a chaplain, was away. We received phone calls, assurances of prayers, balloons, cards, and bouquets of flowers.

These beautiful acts of love would not have happened except for one thing: those who acted in love toward us had to know of our need. When our new friend asked me how she could help, I replied, "Well, my husband says food is always good." Initially embarrassed, he appreciated my forwardness when two weeks' worth of delicious meals appeared in our kitchen! In order to prevent isolation, we may need to pick up the phone or knock on a door and ask for help.

Plugging in to a faith community helps alleviate loneliness. Sometimes we find a church family right away, and sometimes the search takes time. Nonetheless, we make it a priority to begin searching immediately and to keep looking until we find a place of worship. After finding our church home, we look for ways to be involved and begin new friendships.

Loneliness is a common, human emotion. Staying close to Jesus and connecting with others within our community are two certain antidotes in dealing with loneliness.

Ask

When I feel lonely, how do I respond?
Do I isolate myself from God? From others?
How can I connect with other people
within my community and build relationships?

Pray

Lord, When I feel lonely, help me draw close to You. Help me to sense Your presence and hear Your voice speaking to me. Thank You for being my constant companion. I know that having relationships with people involves risk and takes time. Lead me to safe places that will provide new, long-lasting friendships with others. In Jesus' Name, Amen.

by Lori Mumford

SAYING GOOD-BYE *Again*

Show me, O Lord, my life's end and the number of my days; let me know how fleeting is my life. You have made my days a mere handbreadth; the span of my years is as nothing before you. Each man's life is but a breath.

PSALM 39:4–5 NIV

★ ★ ★

THE MOVERS ARE COMING tomorrow, and my mind is racing with all the things that need to be done. For a moment, those thoughts cease while I dwell on the precious brothers and sisters I have to leave. Some I've gotten to know well, and others I've only had the privilege of watching their godly lives. Oh, there's my kindred spirit! Who will I want more to share our traditional ham dinner with before Christmas? Who else will laugh and cry so easily with me? Who else has mannerisms so much like my own that we neither have to explain ourselves? Who else will I humbly watch and learn from? I will miss her.

If I stayed in those thoughts, I would remain hopelessly desperate, but I'm reminded of Psalm 39:4–5. Our lives here are a "mere handbreadth." In fact, even if I live to be a hundred, that is short from an eternal perspective. So, I must say good-bye to these dear ones, knowing that if I don't get to see them again face to face while here on earth, then we haven't long here until we meet again for all eternity.

In 1 Thessalonians 4:16–18 (NIV), it says, "For the Lord himself will come down from heaven, with a loud command, with the voice of the archangel and with the trumpet call of God, and the dead in Christ will rise first. After that, we who are still alive and are left will be caught up together with them in the clouds to meet the Lord in the air. And so we will be with the Lord forever. Therefore encourage each other with these words." When I steer my thoughts to that heavenly promise, I *am* encouraged. He gives me the peace to leave and the will to let go.

God has eternal reasons for bringing all sorts of people in and out of our lives. We might not always understand the whys of His timing, but we must deliberately choose to trust Him. There are locations where He gives us a kindred spirit, and there are locations where He gives none but Himself. Those are the times we must draw nearer to Him, because He uses them to fill us with Himself and to make us a better friend to the next persons He gives us. We will have fewer expectations of people filling our needs where God should. We can trust that He will place new friends in our lives in His perfect timing and for His good purpose.

Ask

When this tour ends, will I dwell on the separation, or will I ask God to give me an eternal perspective for the people He weaves in and out of my life?

Pray

Dear Lord, Thank you for these dear people You've placed in my life during these years. I trust that the next place You take us, You'll give, in Your time, others for us to know and befriend for Your good purpose. You have perfect reasons for meshing our lives together. Let us never forget that our lives are but a breath, so that we may be glad and trust You in our earthly life and rejoice and anticipate our heavenly one. In Jesus' Name, Amen.

by Jocelyn Green

IS GOD *Enough?*

And He has said to me, "My grace is sufficient for you, for power is perfected in weakness."
2 CORINTHIANS 12:9

★ ★ ★

IT IS A FAMILIAR BUT JARRING ROUTINE: A jet goes down. The squadron is shut down, so no calls can go in or out. The Air Force wives and children at home are left to wonder, until the authorities make the announcement, which of them has been widowed, which children will never again see their father. Suppressed fears come boiling up to the surface. How can the military wife ever get used to this?

During her twenty-year marriage to a fighter pilot, *Heroes at Home* author Ellie Kay has supported her family through several deployments and countless training missions. Her husband has survived dozens of emergencies, while some of his friends did not. Even now that he is retired from the Air Force, he still has a dangerous job flying military aircraft as a contractor, testing forty-five-year-old planes and then delivering them to the military. Ellie knows fear, and how to combat it.

Ellie reminds us that the U.S. military forces are the best-trained forces in the world. "In the same way, we need to be the best trained military wives in the world," she says. "We need to train our minds into focusing on life and not death. On truth and not lies. On courage and not fear. When our guys go to war, they compartmentalize away their family. We must do that with fear.

"Early on in marriage, I dealt with my fear by realizing that God was still in control," Ellie continues. "As I focused on the love of God and His provision, and His presence, then there was no room for fear. God planted in my heart that no matter what happens with Bob, our five young children and I will be okay. There comes a point in every military wife's life when she will need to make a decision: Is God enough? Is He big enough to deal with fear of death? Big enough to take care of her and her babies, should the unthinkable happen? The ones who decide God is big enough are the ones who can go on and be an encouragement to other people."

When we feel blinded by the unknowns, when we stagger beneath the weight of the what-ifs, it's critical to dwell not in our fear, but on the One who holds all things in His hands. Carolyn Custis James says:

> God's character is crucial, for there are moments in life when God's goodness and love seem to come under a blackout. No matter how we strain our eyes, we cannot see any good, not a trace of God's love. . . . When faith cannot find something tangible to grasp, we are compelled to fly back to the ark of God's unchanging, unfailing character. But faith will not find much of a foothold here if God is a stranger to us. Faith, in the final analysis, is trusting someone you know, even when you don't always understand what he is doing.[1]

Ask

What biblical promises can I cling to that address my fears?
Who do I know who I might be able to help through her fears?

Pray

Lord, Please help me train my focus on You and Your loving provision for me. Do not let a spirit of fear paralyze me from doing the tasks You have set before me to do. Comfort me with Your promise to never leave me nor forsake me. In Jesus' Name, Amen.

by Jocelyn Green

STRANGERS *Again*

All these died in faith, without receiving the promises, but having seen them and having welcomed them from a distance, and having confessed that they were strangers and exiles on the earth. For those who say such things make it clear that they are seeking a country of their own. And indeed if they had been thinking of that country from which they went out, they would have had opportunity to return. But as it is, they desire a better country, that is, a heavenly one. Therefore God is not ashamed to be called their God; for He has prepared a city for them.

HEBREWS 11:13–16

★ ★ ★

"SO WHERE ARE YOU FROM?" The question seems so simple, and yet for most us in the military, the full answer could take five minutes! After a few months of responding with a list of cities, I finally learned to shorten my answer to, "We just moved from Washington, D.C."

One of the hardest things for me about being in the military has been the inability to stay in one community, put down some roots, and allow attachments to grow. Moving every couple of years (sometimes more often!) keeps me feeling like a stranger on a far too regular basis for my taste.

But here is where we have something in common with the faith heroes of Hebrews 11: Abel, Enoch, Noah, Abraham, Sarah, Isaac, Jacob, Joseph, Moses, and more. All of these "confessed that they were strangers and exiles on the earth" (Hebrews 11:13). Webster's College Dictionary defines "stranger" like this: "an outsider, newcomer or foreigner; a guest or visitor." "Exile" is defined as "a prolonged living away from one's country, community, etc."

In other words, these godly people called themselves outsiders and visitors, living away from their country, which is heaven. Philippians 3:20–21 says, "For our citizenship is in heaven, from which also we eagerly wait for a Savior, the Lord Jesus Christ; who will transform the body of our humble state into conformity with the body of His glory, by the exertion of the power that He has even to subject all things to Himself."

An outsider or visitor does not make attachments to the place he or she visits. This very lack of attachment to the things of the world allowed the heroes of the faith to more fully focus on things of eternal significance. On faith, they, too, left behind family, security, and ordinary life to pursue what God called them to do.

Whether we are newcomers or foreigners at our present duty station, may we always be outsiders in the sense that we form no bonds to this world that would distract us from God's calling in our lives.

The next time you are discouraged with another move, take heart! As the writer of Hebrews said, God is not ashamed to be called your God, and He has prepared a heavenly city for you to call your home forever.

Ask

What earthly thing do I long for right now
that may become a distraction from God?
Can people tell by watching me that my citizenship is in
heaven? Why or why not?

Dear Lord, Thank You for making it easier for me to not form unhealthy attachments to any one place. Show me what it means to be an outsider and visitor on earth while eagerly awaiting the city You have prepared for me to dwell in forever with You. In Jesus' Name, Amen.

by Sara Horn

OVERCOMING *Loneliness*

God is our refuge and strength,
an ever-present help in trouble.
PSALM 46:1 NIV

★ ★ ★

WE'VE ALL FELT LONELY at some point. Active military wives feel it when you leave family and friends for a new duty station where you know no one. National Guard and reservist wives like me get lonely when our husband is gone for his one-weekend a month or two- or three-week training times and your civilian friends can't understand. For all military wives, deployments can bring the meaning of loneliness to a whole new level entirely.

God doesn't want us to be lonely. But He does use loneliness to draw us to Him.

I heard a powerful insight recently that a Navy wife shared about her struggle after losing her husband to the USS *Cole* bombing. As a wife, she had always viewed her husband as the pilot and she the copilot. But when her husband died, her view of herself didn't change. Seven years after his death, she was still the copilot, and with the pilot missing; her plane simply circled and circled again, going nowhere and accomplishing nothing. She was waiting for the pilot (whoever that was) to sit in the pilot's seat and point the plane forward once again.

This mentality can be applied to us, as well. When our pilots are out, we the copilots can often keep everything on auto, unwilling or unable to take the controls ourselves, lest we make a mistake or a decision that the pilot disagrees with. And so our planes fly in limbo—unable to land, unable to see anything but the dark clouds in front of us. A lonely place indeed.

Remember: even if we are faced with piloting ourselves, we are not alone. We have our own portable GPS navigation system—God's Provision and Support!

Consider these promises from God's Word: With God as our fortress, we can never be shaken (Psalm 62:1–2). Jesus will meet us where we are (John 14:18). The Lord will never leave us nor forsake us (Hebrews 13:5).

God is there when we feel like no one is. He will provide opportunities for us to overcome our loneliness, but we must be willing to listen for His voice and then act on those gentle directions He gives us.

Veteran military wives offer several ideas for overcoming loneliness. Some of those include:

1. Attend activities that interest you, and talk with other people.
2. If you're new to the area and don't know anyone, find other newcomers and get a group together.
3. Connect with other military spouses during deployments. (If you don't live near an active post or base, consider finding a military support group online, or look for a military wives support group through a local church or a Wives of Faith group in your area.)

We know from what is written in Genesis that God did not create us to be alone. He loves you and wants your life to be full, enjoying fellowship with Him as well as with others.

Do I see myself as a pilot or a copilot?
How can I learn to sit in the pilot's seat when I need to?
What are some things I can do to lessen
the feelings of loneliness?

Pray

Lord, I know when I feel like no one else is there that I have You to lean on. Give me comfort today and let me know You are there. Help me find friends and others I can walk this journey with. Help me lean on You as my navigator. In Jesus' Name, Amen.

by Jocelyn Green

FATHER TO THE *Fatherless*

A father to the fatherless, a defender of widows,
is God in his holy dwelling.
PSALM 68:5 NIV

★ ★ ★

BEFORE CHAPLAIN CAPT. DANIEL W. HARDIN left his Anchorage, Alaska, home for Iraq, he recorded himself reading his daughter's favorite bedtime stories and saying prayers with her, so she could listen to his voice during his deployment. All the kids had a picture of him in his uniform. With the help of the phone and the Internet, he didn't feel quite so far away. Yet despite their best efforts to stay connected, the fact remained that his wife, Ann, like all other wives left on the home front with their children, had to fill the roles of both parents during deployment.

"Psalm 68:5 gives me strength," says Ann. "God is a father to the fatherless. My kids have a father here on earth, but they know that God is going to be there for them. And God defends the widow, which I think applies to all 'technical' widows whose husbands are deployed. My husband can't be everything for me, but God can. That's a great comfort. Knowing that God loves my children and wants what's best for them more than I do, I trust that He will help me parent them when I'm by myself."

Marshéle Carter Waddell, wife of a Navy SEAL for more than twenty years and mother of three children, addresses this issue in her book *Hope for the Home Front*:

During fatherless times, babysitters and family members and friends are helpful, but no one can enable and replenish me like my heavenly Father. I run to *Him*, relax in *His* arms, and draw on *His* strength daily as I am forced to be both Mom and Dad. He reminds me to teach my children that only one Father is constant, ever present, and all-powerful. I fall to my knees at the end of many days and through tears praise Him that, because of His promises, even a seemingly fatherless childhood will work for each child's good and to His glory. God's Word comforts me. "He defends the cause of the fatherless" and "A father to the fatherless, a defender of widows, is God in his holy dwelling" (Deuteronomy 10:18, Psalm 68:5).[2]

God's promise in Isaiah 40:31 is that "those who hope in the Lord will renew their strength. They will soar on wings like eagles; they will run and not grow weary, they will walk and not be faint." What a relief for solo spouses and "fatherless" kids. No matter how often our men are called away from their homes to serve our country, our source of strength and renewal is anchored in the eternal, unchanging person of Jesus Christ.

Ask

What do I rely on my husband for what I can, instead, draw from my heavenly bridegroom? How can I impress upon my children how much God the Father cares for them?

Pray

Lord, It's so easy to grow weary when I have solo duty. When I am tempted to despair in my own weakness, remind me that I have an unlimited supply of strength, grace (and patience!) in You. Help me rest in Your promise to be a father to the fatherless and a defender of widows. In Jesus' Name, Amen.

by Sara Horn

TRADING FEAR FOR *Faith*

Now faith is being sure of what we hope for
and certain of what we do not see.
HEBREWS 11:1 NIV

★ ★ ★

THERE ARE PLENTY OF FEARS we face as military wives. We fear for our husbands, for our kids, for our extended family and friends; we fear the inevitable deployment, the move, the change in job, the change in the familiar. We fear for our health, for our parents' health, we fear not being there when a family member needs us most. We can fear a lot, can't we?

Dorothy Thompson was an American journalist who was known in the 1930s for her quite public battle against the Nazi German regime. She once said that "only when we are not afraid, do we begin to live."

She was right. Fear is a paralyzing instrument that keeps us from doing what God wants us to do.

During a Bible study I participated in at church, we women were challenged to "trade our fears for faith." As I got in my car after the first session, the phrase stuck with me.

Carefully navigating my car out of the parking lot, I thought about all of the things I was afraid of at that moment. A writing project with some major challenges. Financial worries. The deployment, now just a couple of months away, for which my Navy reservist husband was preparing to leave.

I really did want to trade my fears for faith, except in

my head, it kept coming out "trading faith for fears." That wouldn't work! Finally, I said out loud, "Okay, Lord, I'm trading my FEARS for FAITH." I started listing, out loud to God, all of the fears that were bottled up inside me.

"God, I trade my fear of failure for faith that you're going to help me succeed."

"God, I trade my fear of meeting this deadline for faith that you are going to be my thoughts and my words."

"God, I trade my fear of this deployment for faith that you will be there through the journey."

After I finished listing all of my fears and gave a prayer of thanks to God for honoring those "trades," I was hit with the overwhelming realization that I was driving in a downpour of rain. I hadn't noticed that shortly after I left the church, the rain had started. What was even stranger was that I was completely calm.

One of my greatest fears is driving in the rain—I hate it! But there I was, driving along, my windshield wipers whipping back and forth furiously while I was feeling like the sun was shining and the birds were singing. There was no fear, no nervousness. Instead, I felt calm and peaceful and confident, and I knew that the Holy Spirit was with me. I had traded my fears for faith, and God honored it in the most incredible way by sending His Comforter and Encourager right then.

The next time you feel afraid, stop right where you are and ask God to trade your fear for the faith that only He can give you.

Ask

What am I afraid of today?
What can God replace my fear with instead?

Pray

Lord, I trade my fear of ________________ for the faith that You will ________________________. (List all that come to mind.) Thank You for being our Comforter and Encourager and for taking away our fears when we ask You to. Give me the confidence and the secure knowledge that You are always with me and I have nothing to fear. In Jesus' Name, Amen.

by Marshéle Carter Waddell

THOUGH MY HEART *Quakes...*

I am still confident of this:
I will see the goodness of the Lord in the land of the living.
Wait for the Lord;
Be strong and take heart and wait for the Lord.
PSALM 27:13–14 NIV

★ ★ ★

I CRIED MYSELF TO SLEEP LAST NIGHT. My husband has been told to pack, to prepare to return to war.

And yet, I know God is just as much Lord today as He's been on all my hope-filled days. He is still Lord on this painful, confusing, fearful day. His character, His promises to me, His love for me remain unchanged. Only my circumstances have changed. I keep reminding myself that my joy, my strength, and my hope do not depend on the happenings of my life. My joy, my strength, and my hope are all found in my Lord Jesus, regardless of what is unfolding around me or what lies ahead for me.

Habakkuk, too, experienced fear. When the Lord told Habakkuk that his land would be invaded by a ruthless people, Habakkuk "heard and my inward parts trembled, at the sound my lips quivered. Decay enters my bones, and in my place I tremble" (Habakkuk 3:16). Yet he goes on to utter one of the most beautiful proclamations of faith in the Bible in verses 17–19:

Though the fig tree should not blossom
And there be no fruit on the vines,

Though the yield of the olive should fail
And the fields produce no food,
Though the flock should be cut off from the fold
And there be no cattle in the stalls,
Yet will I exult in the Lord,
I will rejoice in the God of my salvation.
The Lord God is my strength,
And He has made my feet like hinds' feet,
And makes me walk on my high places.

Habakkuk did three things that we can learn from: he told his honest doubts to God, he resolved to wait on God, and he chose to trust God even when he couldn't see the future.

I don't know what your *thoughs* are today, but here are mine: *Though* my husband is returning to war and my heart quakes . . . *Though* I will be a single parent yet again . . . *Though* life continues to throw me curve balls . . . Yet will I trust the Lord God.

Ask

When I am afraid, do I still trust in the Lord
as the blessed and only Sovereign (1 Timothy 6:15)?

Pray

Lord, Thank you that You are totally in control of the decisions the nations' leaders are making presently. I choose not to lean on my own understanding. Bind the ugly spirit of fear from me, from my husband, from our children, from our family and friends. Draw us closer to You through all of this, to hear You, to see You, to serve You better than ever before. And, Lord, when it's all over, may we never revert to the place from which You moved us, grew us, and strengthened us. Help us, at this difficult intersection, to choose to stay on the road You've marked out for us in Your perfect wisdom and love. Use me, Lord, as You see best. Don't allow me to be overcome by fear or paralyzed by hopelessness or anger. Empty me of me and fill me with You. Not mine, but Your will be done. In Jesus' Name, Amen.

by Lori Mumford

NO FEAR IN HIS *Peace*

For I am the Lord, your God, who takes hold of your right hand and says to you, Do not fear; I will help you. Do not be afraid, O worm Jacob, O little Israel, for I myself will help you, declares the Lord, your Redeemer, the Holy One of Israel.
ISAIAH 41:13–14 NIV

★ ★ ★

MY HUSBAND WAS DEPLOYED, and we had recently moved off base. A repairman was in my home, and our conversation led into my husband's work. For whatever reason, I began to get the creeps. I thought, *This stranger knows too much about us. I'm not comfortable with the questions I've just answered.* I quickly said something to show we were protected, so I blurted out, "Well, our dog really pulls through when he has to." There sat my cowardly, golden retriever, leaning into this man's leg, looking up with adoring eyes. The man knew it was a lie. That night as I lay in bed, I listened to all the new creaks and groans of the place and imagined all kinds of horrors that involved this repairman. I prayed in fear and didn't sleep well.

I couldn't shake the spooks for the next few days, and I sought God's Word. It said that He is my Protector and to not fear, for He will rescue me. I struggled with this. Why, then, do bad things happen to His people? Why are they killed, persecuted, or suffer other hardships? How do I find peace when these things still happen to us?

It doesn't appear that the apostles shared my fears. Many suffered horribly, but Paul boasts about his sufferings in 2 Corinthians 11:16–33. He says in 2 Corinthians. 12:10 (NIV), "That is why for Christ's sake, I delight in weaknesses, in insults, in hardships, in persecutions, in difficulties. For when I am weak, then I am strong." Paul rests in God's promise to us. Isaiah 40:29, 31 NIV says, "He gives strength to the weary and increases the power of the weak. But those who hope in the Lord will renew their strength. They will soar on wings like eagles; they will run and not grow weary, they will walk and not be faint."

God doesn't promise that bad things won't befall His children. We *will* go through storms, but He will be with us. The winds *will* rage around us, but He is eager to calm our spirits. Philippians 4:6–7 NIV says, "Do not be anxious about anything, but in everything, by prayer and petition, with thanksgiving, present your requests to God. And the peace of God, which transcends all understanding, will guard your hearts and your minds in Christ Jesus." Ask Him, and He will give you peace.

As I continued to pray, He calmed me and gave me trust. I must give Him my fears, trust that He will never leave me nor forsake me, and believe that His hand will guide me and hold me fast. When I do pass through waters, He will be with me; and when I pass through rivers, they will not sweep over me; and when I walk through fire, I will not be burned (Isaiah 43:2). My Protector will take my hand and will be with me.

Do I let fears of the unknown consume my thoughts?

Pray

Dear Lord, I feel scared about _________. Lord, You say to not be anxious for anything; give all of my worries to You. So, I give this to You, Lord. Help me trust You in everything, and may Your peace guard my heart and mind in Christ Jesus. In Jesus' Name, Amen.

Section Seven

ACTIVE DUTY FAITH:

Leaning on a Faith That Sustains

Now faith is the assurance of things hoped for, the conviction of things not seen.

HEBREWS 11:1

by Jocelyn Green

CHOOSING *Hope*

Now faith is the assurance of things hoped for,
the conviction of things not seen.
HEBREWS 11:1

★ ★ ★

WHAT IS IT THAT YOU HOPE FOR? Perhaps it is the safety of your husband, or for an easy transition after deployment, or for a certain assignment. Or could it be that you have been walking in difficulty for so long that you are finding it difficult to hope at all? If you find that your faith is giving way to doubt, you are not alone.

The theme of hope runs throughout both the Old and New Testaments. Hebrews 11 honors heroes of the faith for righteousness even when they could not see the end result. Verse 11 says, "By faith even Sarah herself received ability to conceive, even beyond the proper time of life, since she considered Him faithful who had promised." If you remember the story as it is told in Genesis, you will recall that Sarah had such a hard time allowing herself to hope that God would keep His promise of giving her a son that she gave her handmaiden Hagar to Abraham to have a son through her. She took the matter into her own hands before the Lord's plan came to fruition. And yet, after she had waited for years, God still kept His promise and allowed her to give birth to Isaac, who would be the father of countless generations.

In our darkest hours, what we believe about God is the

only thing that can sustain us. Our hope should be placed in God's character, not in our outward circumstances. When we have no answers to the "Why" questions, it is our answer to "Who"—our knowledge of God and assurance that He is sovereign—that keeps us going.

"In all of my trials, it has become quite clear that I have a choice," says Army Chaplain wife Rebekah Benimoff. "I could take all my pain and grief and unanswered questions and truthfully, honestly submit them to El-Shaddai, 'The God Who is Sufficient for His People,' or I could choose to turn away from Him and become resentful. I could choose Hope—or I could choose to walk away from hope. How could I choose hopelessness, when there is such HOPE to be found? I find myself crying out to Him, saying, 'God, I cannot do this on my own.' I choose hope despite what I cannot understand. I choose to believe that God is who He says He is, despite what my circumstances are."

Ask

What am I placing my hope in today?
As I wait, what am I learning about who God is?

Pray

Lord, You know my hopes and fears better than I know them myself. Please show me how to rest in the knowledge of Your sovereignty while I wait for my hopes to be fulfilled. Gently guide me to a place where I can rejoice in Your glory no matter what happens in my own circumstances. In Jesus' Name, Amen.

by Rebekah Benimoff

IN THE *Teeth* OF SUFFERING

You, O Lord, keep my lamp burning; my God turns my darkness into light. With your help I can advance against a troop; with my God I can scale a wall . . . his way is perfect . . . He is a shield for all who take refuge in Him. For who is God besides the Lord? and who is the Rock except our God?

PSALM 18:28–31 NIV

★ ★ ★

MY HUSBAND HAD ONLY BEEN HOME a short time from his second deployment to Iraq when he began to deal with the repercussions of the turbulent circumstances he had faced there. We were trying to "re-learn" how to be a family, but because of the emotional healing that needed to happen, our family life was not living up to my expectations.

I felt isolated and lonely in our new assignment. To stretch me even further, my chaplain husband was having a "crisis of faith." He was angry at God for the enormous amounts of suffering he had witnessed. These were difficult dialogues and extremely difficult days. The light at the end of the tunnel was very dim, indeed.

We often deal with the "unknown" of our future. God is building a newer, stronger faith in my husband, and we are looking to Him to rebuild our family identity as well. It is a struggle, but we have a long history of God providing for us, and I know He will continue to provide what we need.

From this experience, I learned a little about what having

faith is—and what it isn't.

Having faith is about relationship . . . not answers. But neither is faith about the absence of questioning. Jesus does not want us to come to Him once we have everything finally resolved. He wants us to choose relationship despite the unanswered questions. Jesus says, "Come to Me, all who are weary and heavy-laden, and I will give you rest" (Matthew 11:28).

Read Paul's testimony in Romans 8:35. Right after this, 9:1–2 NIV tells us that Paul has "great sorrow and unceasing grief in his heart." Is he denying the pain? No. But he is choosing relationship with God in spite of it.

Elisabeth Elliot writes that the love of God "stands in the very teeth of suffering . . . [God] will not necessarily protect us—not from anything it takes to make us like His son. A lot of hammering and chiseling and purifying by fire will have to go into the process."[1]

We often go to Jesus wanting Him to calm the storm. Yet I think that what He really desires is for us to sit in the shadow of His arms in the midst of the storm.

God wants to sift through all of our desires, our pain, and our disappointments. He wants us to be honest with Him about the reality of our suffering—to admit our swirling emotions. And He wants us to draw near to Him so He can carry us through.

Ask

Are there wounded areas in your life that need to be healed?
Are you willing to embrace the grief
and let Him love you through the suffering?

Pray

Lord, When I am afraid of the unknown, teach me to rely on who I know—the One who created all there is. When I am lonely, remind me that You created me for fellowship with You. When I am angry, help me to be honest about it. When I am sad, be my comfort. When I am happy, let me remember that lasting joy is found in You. Restore my hope. Let me never forget that when I am weary and burdened I will find rest in You. In Jesus' Name, Amen.

by Jocelyn Green

Happily EVER AFTER?

Blessed are the poor in spirit, for theirs is the kingdom of heaven; Blessed are those who mourn, for they shall be comforted."
MATTHEW 5:3–4

★ ★ ★

IN JUST ABOUT EVERY ARTISTIC RENDERING of a soldier's homecoming, be it a song, a movie, or a television commercial, we are left with an emotional high that tells us all is well again. But if military wives assume their reunion with their husbands is a fairy-tale ending to their separation, disappointment is almost sure to set in.

"I have seen way too many military wives build up a fantasy in their minds about what life will be like once their husbands are home—and then be destroyed when this fantasy was not a reality," says National Guard wife Mary Whitlock. Mary says the hardest part of war wasn't her husband's deployment; it was when he first came home. His multiple concussions and his exposure to constant combat and chlorine gas resulted in loss of short-term memory and an extremely heightened sense of anxiety, which in turn resulted in frustration and anger.

When author and Navy wife Marshéle Carter Waddell's husband returned from Iraq with only a broken leg, she praised God for his safety. "Now, months later, I sense that his leg is the least of our concerns," she says. "He is healing outwardly, but his soul walks with a limp."

As Marshéle's husband goes through war's aftermath—the

invisible wounds of post-traumatic stress disorder—she and her children have little more than patience, devotion, and hope in their arsenal to help him win this battle on his home turf. She describes the experience this way:

> Life tries to return to what it was before, but can't. He fights against the relentless surf trying to move back to the sandy, safe shore but is drifting further . . . swept out by a current of guilt, memories too painful to speak, questions to difficult to ask, the suffocating guilt of watching others die when he lived instead, the helplessness of not being able to save a friend, the naked ache of being so far from home, from love, from security, living in a dusty hell under fire at all times, fighting for what seemed an ungrateful and divided nation.

In the Old Testament, God was also called "the Lord Who Heals." One of Jesus' many names in the Bible is "Physician," a name well suited for one who performed so many healing miracles on both the physical and spiritual levels. While God works through modern medicine and counseling to heal the war's injuries of body and mind, we can also entrust the healing process directly to Him, the Author of Life itself. As we pray for healing for our spouses, we can also be praying for large doses of patience for ourselves.

Patience is the only thing that keeps Mary's relationship with her husband strong: "When our partners are easily triggered by small things, remember this is not a reaction based on our actions, but their experiences."

Ask

How can I discipline myself to be
more patient with my husband?

This prayer was written by Marshéle Carter Waddell:

Lord, I cannot see the wounds caused by my husband's war-zone experiences, but You can see them. Only You can heal him. Help me to come to You and to trust You to intercede for us when I cannot find the words. I ask for prayer partners who will remember to pray for us, come what may. I need someone to talk with, Lord, someone who has dealt with this before. Please provide godly counsel and direction. In Jesus' Name, Amen.

by Jocelyn Green

Loose Lips SINK SHIPS

But everyone must be quick to hear, slow to speak and slow to anger; for the anger of man does not achieve the righteousness of God.
JAMES 1:19–20

★ ★ ★

THE PHRASE "LOOSE LIPS MIGHT SINK SHIPS" was coined as a slogan during WWII as part of the U.S. Office of War Information's attempt to limit the possibility of troops inadvertently giving useful information to enemy spies through letters or conversations. We can all understand the importance of censoring certain intelligence so as not to give the enemy an advantage. But even today, deployed soldiers and sailors are not the only ones who need to watch what they say to avoid harmful consequences.

As military wives, what we choose to share with our husbands can encourage or discourage them to the point of distraction. During these times, it is more important for us to remain supportive than to vent our frustrations.

As a new Coast Guard wife, this was a hard pill for me to swallow. There were times when I fought against the depression that seemed to be descending upon me like the long Alaska winter nights I was experiencing for the first time, and I wanted my husband to know about it! Then I learned that when another Coast Guard wife had a miscarriage and her husband was at sea as the commanding officer, she didn't tell him. She grieved alone until her husband returned. My shock must have been written on my face. "If I had told him, he would have been distracted from his job," she told me. "If he makes a mistake out there, people get hurt." It was as simple as that.

Another Coastie wife told me that when phone calls became consistently strained, she and her husband agreed to go without voice-to-voice and stick with e-mail, so they could choose their words more carefully.

Taming the tongue is no small task, but mission critical both for the military spouse and for godly living in general. James says, "If anyone does not stumble in what he says, he is a perfect man, able to bridle the whole body as well. . . . See how great a forest is set aflame by such a small fire! And the tongue is a fire, the very world of iniquity" (James 3:2, 5–6).

"When you speak to your spouse, tell him the positive things but don't go into stressful aspects," says National Guard wife Mary Whitlock. "They need to know you are there for him and support him. It's more important than any feelings you may have. You want to keep his mind clear to focus on his mission."

Ask

Who can I lean on in my community so I'm not tempted to fill my husband's ears with my struggles? How can I communicate support to my husband next time we talk?

Pray

Lord, When I am alone, it is so easy to dwell on my own hardships. Help me discipline myself to take these burdens first to You, and then to a trusted friend, family member, or pastor. May my own trials never add to the stress my husband already endures. In Jesus' Name, Amen.

by Marshéle Carter Waddell

WHEN THE LORD *Takes Away*

The Lord gave and the Lord has taken away.
May the name of the Lord be praised.
JOB 1:21 NIV

★ ★ ★

WOW! IT'S BEAUTIFUL, I thought. An early morning's gentle wave swirled around my sand-sugared ankles and revealed a tiny treasure near my toes. A perfectly spiraled shell rested on the settling sand just beneath the sparkling surface of the water. The sea had chosen me to be the recipient of its prize gift this glorious morning. My soul smiled. *It's all mine*, I thought. I leaned. I reached.

The perfect moment was interrupted by a wave. Ocean and sand frothed, grabbed my gift, and swallowed my treasure. I waited for the next wave to return what was mine, but only the memory of its beauty remained, the artistic mastery of its Creator. Only the undeserved blessing of enjoying it for a moment, however brief, was mine to keep.

Most likely, the vast majority of us will become widows, whether or not death comes through military service. The U.S. Census Bureau tells us that nine out of ten women will experience widowhood for at least some portion of their lives. When our husbands pass on, only the memory of their beauty remains, only the artistic mastery of their Creator. Only the undeserved blessing of enjoying life with them, however brief, is ours to keep.

Hannah felt this way about her son Samuel, for whom she had desperately petitioned the Lord. When the time came for her to give up her small, precious son to be raised at the temple, she thankfully testified to the Lord's rule in life and death. "The Lord kills and makes alive; He brings down to Sheol and raises up" (1 Samuel 2:6). She was thankful for the gift while she had it.

Mary of Nazareth also knew what it was to experience God's greatest gifts and to watch them disappear. Carolyn Custis James notes that at the foot of the cross, "Her marriage was over, and her son was gone too. But she still knew who she was. She was the blessed disciple—firmly ensconced as a sister and a mother in the growing family of Jesus. She was at peace. Her life hadn't turned out as she expected, but her identity and mission were intact."[2]

When the time comes, may we take our cues from these women of faith. May we remain rooted in the Giver and Taker of Life even though we grieve. And in the meantime, may we recognize the incredible gifts that God is allowing us to experience in the people we hold dear.

Ask

Am I pursuing knowledge of and relationship with God now so that when death turns my world upside down, I can still cling to my God?

Pray

Lord, Thank you for this day. Help me to be present in this day, not pining for yesterday and not longing for or dreading tomorrow. Help me to be present, focused, tuned in to Your voice today. As friends speak with me today, help me to genuinely listen and not be a million miles away mentally. Open my eyes to see the soul-level needs of my husband and children today. I ask You for insight and the creativity to speak into their lives just the right words of encouragement and truth. Move my hands to touch them and my arms to hold them close. Life is so fragile, Lord, and so brief. I know all my loved ones belong to you and that their lives are in Your hand. Help me to handle every moment I have with them with deep reverence and gratitude. In Jesus' Name, Amen.

by Ronda Sturgill

THE GIFT OF *Grace*

But by the grace of God I am what I am
and his grace to me was not without effect.
1 CORINTHIANS 15:10 NIV

★ ★ ★

"RONDA, HOW DO YOU GO ABOUT LIVING YOUR LIFE in a wheelchair? Everything you do is so hard, but you make it look so easy." If there is one question people have consistently asked me during the many years I have used a wheelchair, this is it.

Always eager to bring glory and honor to God, I quote the apostle Paul: "By the grace of God I am what I am and his grace to me was not without effect" (1 Corinthians 15:10 NIV).

When my husband was praying about becoming a military chaplain, it was grace that led him to the Air Force. When he spent a year in Korea, it was God's grace that enabled me to live that year without him. When we hear of a new next assignment that is not on our dream sheet, it's grace that enables us to pack up and go. Grace affects every area of our lives.

A delayed flight resulted in my arriving at the gate of a connecting flight just in time to board the plane before the doors closed. The flight attendant insisted I transfer into an empty first-class seat rather than work my way through the very full plane to find my seat in the economy section. Once in the air, the attendant treated me as if I was any other first-class passenger who had paid full price for their ticket. She offered me the first-class meal, along with all the other first-class amenities. Feeling extremely undeserving, I was reluctant at first to accept such treatment. But as she laid my meal tray in front of me, she clearly received joy from giving me something I did not pay for. Amazed, I realized God had just given me a picture of His grace.

God's grace is not something we buy or deserve. It's given to us freely without condition, paid for by Jesus. Grace is not about what we do for God, but rather what God does for us. God gives it abundantly, but we must accept it. Just as the flight attendant wanted me to accept this meal, God wants us to accept his grace.

My favorite definition of grace comes from Strong's concordance: *the merciful kindness by which God, exerting his holy influence upon souls, turns them to Christ, keeps, strengthens, increases them in the Christian faith, knowledge, affection, and kindles them to the exercise of the Christian virtues."* [3] God's grace is always at work within us.

As military wives, we experience God's merciful kindness when our husbands are deployed. Second Corinthians 12:9 tells us, "My grace is sufficient for you, for my power is made perfect in your weakness." He gives us the strength and stamina to take care of our children, He brings friends into our lives to help keep us grounded in the Word, He gives us wisdom as we tend to the affairs of the household, He brings mentors into our lives who teach us new and creative ways of dealing with the separation from our husbands.

The key to experiencing grace is simple: accept it. Ladies, are you accepting the grace God is lavishing upon you? He wants you to have it. He longs for you to have it. He exists to give it to you. Receive it and be blessed!

Have I accepted God's grace in my life?
How have I allowed Him to give me all that He wants to give me?

Pray

Dear Lord, Help me to recognize Your grace working in every area of my life. When I see You, help me to accept what You want to give me. You know I don't deserve it, but You give it to me anyway. My ticket has been purchased and my first-class meal has been paid for. Thank You! In Jesus' Name, Amen.

by Jocelyn Green

ALREADY *Written*

And in Your book were all written
The days that were ordained for me,
When as yet there was not one of them.
PSALM 139:16

★ ★ ★

WHEN MARY WHITLOCK'S husband was deployed to the notoriously dangerous red zone of Ramadi, Iraq, with the Indiana National Guard, she would tell herself three little words to keep her fears for his safety at bay: It's already written. "Whether they are at home or abroad, God's plan for us is already written; we cannot do anything to change it!" she says.

In my conversations with military wives for this book, those who have been able to silence the nagging "what-ifs" concerning the welfare of their husbands remember that God has numbered each of our days. No military mission will interfere with His plans. Job said, "I know that You can do all things, and that no purpose of Yours can be thwarted" (Job 42:2).

In *Hope for the Home Front*, Marshéle Carter Waddell says: "The number of [my husband] Mark's days were ordained, determined before one of them came to be, regardless if he is a gunslinger or if he sits behind a desk and pushes papers. The number and quality of my days are equally in His loving control. Mark's job *is* demanding and dangerous. The amount of danger he faces, however, in no way alters God's sovereignty.

In contrast, it serves to keep my will on the altar."[4]

In Jeremiah, the Lord paints a picture of the difference between trusting in our own strength and resting in God's sovereignty. "Thus says the Lord, 'Cursed is the man who trusts in mankind and makes flesh his strength, and whose heart turns away from the Lord. For he will be like a bush in the desert and will not see when prosperity comes, but will live in stony wastes in the wilderness, a land of salt without inhabitant. Blessed is the man who trusts in the Lord and whose trust is the Lord. For he will be like a tree planted by the water, that extends its roots by a stream and *will not fear when the heat comes*; but its leaves will be green, and it *will not be anxious in a year of drought nor cease to yield fruit*" (Jeremiah 17:5–8, emphasis added). What an incredible promise!

Isaiah 41:10 declares, "Do not fear, for I am with you; do not anxiously look about you, for I am your God. I will strengthen you, surely I will help you, surely I will uphold you with My righteous right hand." We can only trust God when our focus is on Him and not on our circumstances.

Psalm 112:7 says, "He will not fear evil tidings; his heart is steadfast, trusting in the Lord." As our hearts are fixed on our sovereign, loving Lord, we can be at peace in the midst of unknowns.

Ask

Am I trusting in mankind or is my trust in the Lord Himself?

Pray

Lord, Remind me that our days were numbered even before we were born. I desperately desire to trust fully in You, to be like a tree planted by the water, rooted in the life-giving waters that come only from You. Help me train my heart and mind to trust in Your sovereignty. In Jesus' Name, Amen.

by Sheryl Shearer

THE STING OF *Death*

O death, where is your sting?
1 CORINTHIANS 15:55

★ ★ ★

STATIONED IN HAWAII at the time, we boarded a C-130 military hop in mid-October, leaving gorgeous, balmy Honolulu, landing eight hours later in the great frozen tundra of Grand Forks AFB, North Dakota. The plan was a two-week family visit at my parents' home in Minnesota and then a prompt exodus back to paradise. Those plans were quickly cancelled when we found out my dad had stage-four lung cancer.

Throughout the next three months, our family watched this devastating disease slowly debilitate his body and turn our lives upside down. Being a part of military life, I am used to sudden changes, but having no experience with serious illness, cancer, or death, I entered unknown territory. As a stoic person, I often masked my feelings to outsiders. I provided updates to our military community in Hawaii, omitting any hint of my emotional turmoil. Yet when I was alone, my prayers often consisted of tears and petitions to God.

At night, I lay in bed sobbing, pleading with God to heal his body. I worried about the grief my daughters were experiencing at such young ages. I mourned the loss of "normal." I grieved at not being able to return to Hawaii and say good-bye to our military friends and church family. I ached to see the physical pain my dad suffered and the emotional pain my mom faced with the loss of her life partner. Mostly, I agonized over my father's spiritual relationship with God.

When death knocks on one's door, spiritual concerns take precedence. Our mortality has a way of crystallizing the important issues of life. Faced with the uncertainty of his own mortality, my dad began to ask spiritual questions and actually listen to the responses. At the end of his days he opened his heart to God's grace, acknowledging his need for God's forgiveness. "How do I know for certain?" he asked. "You have to trust God as being truthful and honest. If God says something, then God means it," I replied. After much thought, he accepted God's promise by faith.

Even though I know that my dad has the ultimate victory, the sting of death still pricks my heart. Birthdays, anniversaries, pictures, no more phone calls, and his favorite things—the Navy and flying airplanes—hurt. The eternal hope of seeing him again provides comfort and I say with thanks and confidence, "Death is swallowed up in victory . . . but thanks be to God, who gives us the victory through our Lord Jesus Christ" (1 Corinthians 15:54, 57).

Ask

Am I willing to sacrifice things in my own life
to help a loved one?
Is there a loved one in my life that does not have assurance of eternal life that I can pray for, give a call, or send a card to?

Pray

Lord God, Help me to grieve my loss. Thank You for taking the sting of death away and providing hope and comfort in death. Help me to be a part of carrying the gospel to my friends and loved ones. Show me how I can connect with them and be a reflection of You. In Jesus' Name, Amen.

by Rebekah Benimoff

Faith CHALLENGED

You hear O Lord, the desire of the afflicted;
you encourage them, and you listen to their cry.
PSALM 10:17 NIV

★ ★ ★

WHEN A YOUNG LADY who once served on the chapel praise team with me learned that her husband had been killed in Iraq, those of us who served with her were shaken. While some people I knew were certain that God had told them everything would be okay, I had no such assurance. What God told me was quite different. He said that no matter what happens, He would carry me through. And to this day, He has.

Romans 8:28 NIV says, "We know that in all things God works for the good of those who love him, who have been called according to his purpose." God can take any circumstance—anything that seems terrible at the time, and use it for His purposes. No matter how far I fall, no matter how huge my disappointment, whether life knocks me on my rear or on my face, God can and WILL redeem it. Nothing is beyond His reach. No burden so heavy, no circumstance so bad that He cannot transform it into something for the good of HIS Kingdom.

It is not for me to make sense of seemingly senseless tragedy, but simply to submit to what the Holy Spirit can teach me through the struggle—to go to Him for healing, and trust Him with the rest. Faith is believing in God's character . . . trusting Him to bring that GOOD to pass when all I see is the storm.

From my journey with my husband, I am already learning a few things . . .

When someone is struggling with their faith, don't say simply, "Oh, God has a plan, it will all work out." Allow the person to walk through the trials so that his or her faith can be tested and refined.

When the wound is raw, put aside your own discomfort and your own desire to have an answer, and just BE with the person. When my husband says something that flies in the face of the picture I have of God, I have to discipline myself to listen only and not correct what I think is an inaccurate picture of God.

I have learned that the desire to correct is really my own discomfort with what he is saying. My own faith is being challenged. The tendency is to glaze over that, but I have to be alert to why I feel the need to correct, and discipline myself to simply listen, and not spout off an answer.

As Elisabeth Elliot writes, "However it is of no use measuring suffering. What matters is making the right use of it, taking advantage of the sense of helplessness it (suffering) brings to turn one's thoughts to God. . . . Trust IS the lesson."[5]

Ask

Is there a circumstance in your life that you
have believed to be beyond God's ability
or willingness to redeem?
What are you believing about God
and/or His character that is holding you back
from total surrender?

Pray

Lord, There are times when life is so out of our control that we forget that You have a plan and a purpose for each of us. When our faith is shaken or challenged, teach us to seek truth in Your character and promises. Let us never forget Your great love for us. Teach us to say with certainty that the cross is ***enough!*** *And let us always remember that the power that raised Jesus Christ from the dead is the same power that we can claim to walk victoriously and seek truth. In Jesus' Name, Amen.*

by Pamela Anderson

Abide WITH ME

I am the vine, you are the branches;
he who abides in Me, and I in him, he bears much fruit;
for apart from Me you can do nothing.
JOHN 15:5

★ ★ ★

I CHERISH AND REVEL in my role as mother, but as I stare directly into the face of my husband's upcoming deployment, it gives me pause. For the next seven months I alone, humanly speaking, will be completely responsible for my daughter's emotional, physical, and spiritual welfare, not to mention our finances, house, car, and Finn the fish. And I don't just want to survive, I want the next seven months to be fruitful in my life and my daughter's.

Clearly, I am not the first woman to face lengthy separation from my husband for the sake of country. I am surrounded by these unsung heroes in the aisles of the commissary and the exchange, and these women are only the latest links forged in a chain of brave and uncommon sisters extending back to the infancy of our nation. Abigail Adams, wife of our second president and a patriot in her own right, endured several separations, some lasting years, from her husband, John, as he served in the Continental Congress and later as ambassador to France. Abigail oversaw their farm and orchards, as well as all household functions, saw to the education and discipline of the Adams children, tended to their financial affairs, hired and managed servants, supplied food and drink to American soldiers, sheltered patriot families fleeing Boston, and accomplished it all during a time when goods were in short supply and the danger from the British imminent. Talk about being fruitful!

In the John 15 passage quoted above, God in Christ is pictured as the vine and I am assigned my appropriate role as the branch. Apart from that eternal, omnipotent, life-giving vine, I can do nothing.

Over the seven months of my husband's deployment I will need God's strength to produce the fruit I desperately want to grow in my life: unconditional love for a child whose heart yearns for her daddy; true joy when a friend's husband returns and I have many months of separation left to endure; peace when the nightly news reports danger and casualties near my husband's location; patience and kindness when my daughter asks for the hundredth time in a day, "What time is it where Daddy is?"; goodness and faithfulness in heart and deed to the man I married and our shared dreams; gentleness and self control when I feel like hurling my frustrations at the nearest available target. These are the fruits I desire, but fruitfulness comes only as I abide in Christ, the vine, and, wonder of wonders, He abides in me.

The Greek word for abide is *mĕnō*, meaning to remain, dwell, and in this particular instance the idea of persevering. I remain with Christ, Christ remains with me. I dwell with Christ, and Christ dwells with me. I persevere in my weakness to abide in the vine, the glorious vine perseveres in His strength and abides in me. I live as a branch securely attached to the vine, our intimate attachment my first thought at dawn, the last whisper of my spirit each night, my shield and defender for each breath in between.

Am I making a conscious effort
to abide in the Vine each day?
How can I grow more intimately
attached to Christ?

Pray

"Abide with me; fast falls the eventide;
The darkness deepens; Lord with me abide!
When other helpers fail, and comforts flee,
Help of the helpless, O abide with me.
I need Thy presence ev'ry passing hour;
What but Thy grace can foil the tempter's power?
Who, like Thyself, my guide and stay can be?
Through cloud and sunshine, Lord, abide with me."
—Henry Lyte[6]

Section Eight

HOPE OF VICTORY:

Recognizing God's Goodness

Yet those who wait for the Lord
will gain new strength;
They will mount up with wings like eagles,
They will run and not get tired,
they will walk and not become weary.

ISAIAH 40:31

by Paulette Harris

ARE YOU *Ready?*

Therefore, prepare your minds for action; be self-controlled; set your hope fully on the grace to be given you when Jesus Christ is revealed.

1 PETER 1:13 NIV

★ ★ ★

MANY TIMES our husbands are called out at the last minute. During Desert Storm, my husband had his bags packed by the door due to "stand-by," which meant he could be called any time, night or day. It is sometimes a hard life but if we are prepared to meet these circumstances, it makes it a lot easier for our families. We have talks often and share as much as we can with our family so that things aren't such a surprise when we have to change or move to a new location. We try to make it fun and a part of life.

The most wonderful observation that I learned in my Bible studies is that just as we are called to prepare to go at any moment, there is preparation going on for us at the other end.

When we call our families and tell them we are coming for a visit, they get excited to see us; sometimes it has been two or three years since our last visit in person. Relatives get in on the action, and by the time we arrive, things are in order for fun and celebration.

But that's nothing compared to the glory that awaits us in heaven! Listen to this: "However, as it is written: 'No eye has seen, no ear has heard, no mind has conceived what God has prepared for those who love Him' but God has revealed it to us by his Spirit" (1 Corinthians 2:9 NIV).

How exciting is that? God our Father has a place that is prepared, waiting for us when we come home. Not only has Jesus prepared a place for us to come home to, but He is equipping us to get ready for that wonderful reunion in heaven. That's the love of our Father—He always helps us if we ask.

My favorite Scripture for becoming prepared in Jesus is 2 Timothy 4:1–2 (NIV): "In the presence of God and of Christ Jesus, who will judge the living and the dead, and in view of his appearing and his kingdom, I give you this charge: Preach the Word; be prepared in season and out of season; correct, rebuke and encourage—with great patience and careful instruction."

As much as I love going home to see my family, I joyfully anticipate the homecoming in heaven when I finally see my heavenly Father face to face. Even as Jesus is preparing that place for us, may we also be preparing our hearts and minds according to 2 Timothy 4:1–2.

Ask

What am I doing to prepare to go home?
Am I studying God's Word to find out what
He needs me to do to prepare to meet Him?

Pray

Lord, I am so glad You have thought of everything. You care about me and my daily walk with You. You are preparing a place for me, and I feel so loved and special. I want Your help to prepare me to meet You and come home in your timing. Give me strength and courage to walk uprightly until that wonderful day. Give my family strength as we move according to Your will from place to place, remembering that You always provide a family for us. Bless those we leave behind as we move forward. In Jesus' Name, Amen.

by Jocelyn Green

FULFILLING *Time*

For we are His workmanship,
created in Christ Jesus for good works, which God
prepared beforehand so that we would walk in them.
EPHESIANS 2:10

★ ★ ★

I KNOW WHY MY HUSBAND IS HERE. BUT WHY AM I HERE? The question haunted me as a new military wife.

With the transfer from Washington, D.C., to the small town of Homer, Alaska, Rob's career advanced; mine seemed cut off. I struggled to find a new purpose to call my own. It was easy to invest in a supportive role when Rob was home, but when he was at sea, I simply filled time. It took me a while to truly *fulfill* time by discovering what God would have me do.

Patti Morse, an Air Force wife of more than twenty-five years, speaks to all of us who ache to know God has a purpose for us when she says, "God created me and prepared specific good works beforehand which I am to walk in to bring Him glory on this earth. So when I wake up alone in a foreign country where I cannot understand or speak the language and my husband is gone and all family and friends are far away . . . I remember that it is GOD who has placed me here—not the military—and I am here for a very specific purpose which God has ordained!"

When Ellie Kay married her fighter pilot husband, she left a successful business as a broker. Yet when she put all of her skills and experience to work paying off her family's debt and sharing her methods with other military families, God blessed her work and ministry. Now, with twelve books in print and opportunities to travel the world, she is known as America's Family Financial Expert. Ellie Kay is fulfilling God's purpose for her!

Not all of us will make the news when we do what God calls us to do, but we can all be sure that God does indeed have a plan for us. Carolyn Custis James says:

> A married woman faces a . . . problem when she believes the plan she's on belongs to her husband. Her plan seems eclipsed by God's plan for him. . . . She braces herself for his next big decision and the adjustments she will have to make. . . . When someone asks a married woman why she moved to town, nine times out of ten she will say it is because God brought her husband to such and such a job, and plenty of seminary wives and women on the mission field justify their presence by saying, "God led my husband here." I understand what they mean, but it troubles me that so few women have any inkling that God relocated them because it was His plan for her. It's hard to have a clear sense of purpose or calling if you're convinced you're only tagging along.
>
> God has a unique plan for each woman. We are called not to sit on the sidelines but to be players, active contributors, to run the race He has marked out for us. If God is sovereign, then every day of our lives has meaning and purpose because God has planned it. We are not left in the wake of God's plan for someone else. No matter how intertwined our lives become with the lives of husbands, friends, and family members, God's plan for us is individual and personal.[1]

How have I seen God orchestrating my life
for His glory and my good?
What might God's purpose be for me
in my current situation?

Pray

Lord, Thank You for creating a perfect plan for my life. Help me to see Your hand moving through our circumstances. May I be filled with Your grace and strength to do today what You have ordained for me to do. In Jesus' Name, Amen.

by Ronda Sturgill

COMPLETE IN *Christ*

For in Christ all the fullness of the Deity lives in bodily form, and you have been given fullness in Christ.
COLOSSIANS 2:9,10 NIV

★ ★ ★

THE PHONE CALL I HAD BEEN DREADING for four years came suddenly. Saddam Hussein had just invaded Kuwait. My husband had less than twelve hours to pack and get to the departure location for his deployment. In the early morning hours of August 8, 1990, I heard the squeal of a C5 taking off and knew he was on that plane headed for the other side of the world. My heart began to sink. I had no idea where he was going or when he'd ever be back. I was left all by myself to raise our six-year-old son.

Although a first for an experience such as this, I am used to facing life's challenges. When I was eighteen years old I became a paraplegic as the result of a horseback riding accident. At the time of this writing I have used a wheelchair for mobility for thirty-two years. I learned from a very early age there is nothing we have that cannot be taken away from us. The only thing we have that cannot be taken away from us is our relationship with Jesus Christ.

In his letter to the Colossians, Paul repeatedly tells the people of Colossae they are complete in Christ. Questioning the gospel Paul was preaching, they were determined to add to this gospel. They were being told they needed more than Jesus Christ.

Today in our Western culture, we live in a society that also tells us we need more than Jesus: more clothes, bigger houses, luxury cars, more television stations, more cell phones . . . and we all need to look at least ten years younger, don't we?

How easy it is for us to buy into this way of thinking. When we are faced with the difficulties of daily life, we become extremely vulnerable to the world and its hollow and deceptive philosophies. Paul tells us if we are not careful, we will be taken captive. To be taken captive means to be taken as a prisoner, to be held in bondage. This is exactly what happens to us when we look to things other than Christ to make us complete.

Because I am complete in Christ, I can love my husband unconditionally. This unconditional love allows me to support him in his military career, no matter what that brings: four moves in four years, long and dangerous duty assignments, single parenting. The list goes on and on. I am complete in Christ and it is He who meets all my needs. Not my husband, not my children, and certainly not the world in which I live.

Ladies, stay rooted and established in your faith. Study consistently, pray fervently, and praise God often for the life He has given you. It's an honor to stand by our husbands as they protect the freedoms this country gives each and every one of us. I'll never be able to wear a uniform and go to war, but I can stay home and take care of my household while my husband goes. And I can do that because I am complete in Christ.

Ask

In what ways do I find my completeness in Christ?
What is the evidence of my answer?

Pray

Dear Lord, Thank you that I am complete in You. You are all I need. You will supply all my needs according to Your riches in glory. I love my husband, but I cannot find in him the completeness that I find in You. Draw me closer to You this week, I pray. In Jesus' Name, Amen.

by Lori Mumford

THE PROPER *Time*

The wise heart will know the proper time and procedure. For there is a proper time and procedure for every matter . . .
ECCLESIASTES 8:5–8 NIV

★ ★ ★

WHILE WE WERE STATIONED in Kodiak, Alaska, my mother was diagnosed with a fatal lung disease that would take her life in a few years unless a miracle happened. As her disease progressed, I worried about getting home to her. I often prayed to God: if it be Your will, let me know the proper time to help my dad with her. It wasn't easy to pack up and go to them. They lived three thousand miles away, and my husband was often gone on a Coast Guard boat, leaving me alone with three children.

I'll never forget my phone conversation with Mom just after Christmas.

"Mom, will you please tell me if you think you need me there. You and Dad always say that everything is fine."

With labored breathing, she said, "Well, I'll try. We'll have to talk more about that, honey. Can I call you back? Your cousin is here with me while your dad made a quick run to the grocery store."

"Mom, does someone need to stay there with you while Dad goes to the store?"

"Yes, I've started feeling really anxious without him."

With those words, I immediately knew what to do

through the Holy Spirit.

"Mom, I think it's time for me to come home and help."

The Lord worked out our finances and my husband's schedule with our children. I arrived at my parents' house, and my mother died just two weeks later. "My times are in Your hands . . . " (Psalm 31:15 NIV). "There is a time for everything, and a season for every activity under heaven: a time to be born and a time to die" (Ecclesiastes 3:1 NIV).

Many military families live far away from loved ones who need us, and even in His will, we're unable to attend our loved ones' funerals, birthdays, weddings, and graduations. These are the times when you are tempted to doubt the purpose of your transient life. When we're absent from these occasions, ask Him for rest in His will. In sickness and death, He will "comfort all who mourn and provide for those who grieve . . . " (Isaiah 61:2, 3 NIV). Matthew 5:4 NIV says, "Blessed are those who mourn, for they will be comforted." There is no comfort that outlasts His.

On the other hand, when the Lord wills that you return to family, every person's cue will not necessarily be the same. Rather, the Holy Spirit will uniquely prompt you and show you what steps to take when we ask for wisdom, give Him our worries, and put the situation in His hands. As a military spouse, may you never forget that as He has determined set times and exact places for nations, He also has determines them for you (Acts 17:26–27).

Ask

Do I worry about living far from loved ones when the difficulty and expense of returning to them is great?

Dear Lord, Only You know our futures. I have no power over any of it, but You do. Praise You, Father. You say in Proverbs 16:4 that You work out everything for Your own end. Verse 9 says that in my heart, I plan my course, but You, Lord, "determine my steps." Now, take my worries and let me rest in Your peace that if it is Your will, You will let me know when it is time to help loved ones or to rejoice with them. And You will provide me with the way and the means to get there. Thank You. In Jesus' Name, Amen.

by Vanessa Peters

TIMES AND *Seasons*

There is a time for everything,
and a season for every activity under heaven:
. . . a time to plant and a time to uproot . . .
ECCLESIASTES 3:1–2 NIV

★ ★ ★

WHEN I SERVED AS THE WELCOME CHAIR for our squadron, it was my job to bring information packets, brownies, and a warm smile to new families on the base. I'd usually show up at a TLF (Temporary Living Facility) or VOQ (Visiting Officer's Quarters) to greet the newcomers. Not only were they new to the base, but many were serving their first permanent assignment. They usually were starved for friendship, and gobbled up any morsel of information about the area, the base, or the squadron. One thing I always shared was that it usually took about six months before they'd feel comfortable and "at home" in their new surroundings. They'd nod, but you could see in their eyes that it sounded like an eternity. They were thirsting for normalcy, fellowship, and the feeling of home.

Now we live out in the country, surrounded by wildlife. We've just experienced a particularly harsh winter, and it's a wonder any animals survived it. Our family is astonished by the two rabbits that live outside our kitchen window in a little thicket of trees. They exhibit a fierce tenacity to survive. Most evenings, I see them venture out from their burrow to seek nourishment, though the pickings are slim at this time of year.

I find myself anxious for spring on their behalf, so they can feast on rich grass.

As military wives, we are a bit like those bunnies in my backyard. Sometimes we experience bleak "winters" where our friends and comforts are sparse. Often, this occurs just after a move, or when our friends are reassigned. But God is gracious, and other seasons are rich with abundance. God will provide a soul mate at just the right time, or a neighbor who warms our hearts.

Christians have been given the "secret" of making it through the seasons of life. The apostle Paul says, "I have learned to be content whatever the circumstances. I know what it is to be in need, and I know what it is to have plenty. I have learned the secret of being content in any and every situation . . . whether living in plenty or in want. I can do everything through him who gives me strength" (Philippians 4:11–13 NIV).

This advice is credible and poignant coming from a man who survived shipwrecks, persecution, imprisonment, and beatings—and, incidentally, who was always on the move and physically separated from those he loved most. God wants us to lean on Him no matter what our circumstances. We can't simply muster up the willpower to survive; we are strengthened by a Savior of infinite power.

If we never experienced the difficult times, we would be hard-pressed to relate to others when they face similar trials. And we would not fully appreciate the times of abundance if we did not face periods of scarcity. God grants times and seasons in our lives for a reason, and His grace will sustain us through them all. If you feel like a rabbit searching for a bit of dead grass, take heart. Spring is on its way!

Ask

Do I trust God's grace to sustain me
when I am facing loneliness?
Do I share in the sufferings of others when
they are going through a rough season?

Pray

God, I know there are times and seasons for the military wife. Help me to lean on You in the dry patches, and thank You when fellowship and comforts abound. In Jesus' Name, Amen.

by Sara Horn

REMEMBERING *God's Grace*

But he said to me, "My grace is sufficient for you, for my power is made perfect in weakness." Therefore I will boast all the more gladly about my weaknesses, so that Christ's power may rest on me.

2 CORINTHIANS 12:9 NIV

★ ★ ★

IT WAS A WARM SUMMER DAY and the new school year was just a week away. While my husband was serving with his fellow Seabees in Iraq, my son Caleb and I were getting his room ready—sorting out toys he no longer played with and clothes he could no longer wear. Then it was time to sort the marker bag.

The marker bag has been with us probably longer than Caleb has been alive. It's a mixture of pens and markers, things I used in my scrapbooking and craft-making days. Caleb inherited it for coloring but I knew there were a lot of markers in there that didn't work. I pulled out an old scrap of paper, and Caleb and I sat down on the floor of his room to sort the good ones from the bad.

As our system developed—pick up the marker, take the cap off, scratch a doodle on the paper—Caleb and I took turns saying "weak" or "this one's good" as we threw the markers in the respective containers. The stronger markers stayed; the weak ones got the trash bag.

Aren't you glad God doesn't do that to us? There have been

so many times in life, particularly during our recent deployment, when I felt so close to being dried up. I was so tired and so weary of being the one holding it all together; taking care of the house, caring for our little boy, being the encourager to my husband on the other side of the world. I wasn't bursting with color; I was barely making a mark. But God in His incredible way always knows how to infuse me; how to strengthen me; how to bring me back to the original condition He created me to be.

If there is anything I have learned from this deployment, it's that God is glorified the most when we can only do the least.

He isn't expecting perfection. Remember, when God created the universe and everything in it, he called it "very good"—not "perfect"—and was pleased.

God simply asks for our obedience. Our availability. Ourselves. God loves us just as we are. There is nothing more and nothing less we can do to achieve His love because it is a gift. All we are asked to do is receive it.

Be grateful for grace today. God's given you a permanent place in the marker bag.

Ask

In what ways am I trying to be perfect
where I don't need to be?
How can I remind myself daily
of God's grace and love for me?

Pray

Lord, Thank You for loving me as I am with imperfections, shortcomings, and weaknesses. Help me be mindful that I don't have to earn Your love; You give it freely. Help me receive it with open arms and a heart full of gratitude. In Jesus' Name, Amen.

by Eathel Weimer

THE *Fall*—A SEASON

Therefore, I urge you, brothers, in view of God's mercy, to offer your bodies as living sacrifices, holy and pleasing to God—this is your spiritual act of worship. Do not conform any longer to the pattern of this world, but be transformed by the renewing of your mind. Then you will be able to test and approve what God's will is—His good, pleasing and perfect will.
ROMANS 12:1–2 NIV

★ ★ ★

WITH MY COFFEE CUP IN HAND, I stepped out onto the front porch of our rented retreat cabin in the woods for my devotional time. While sitting in the stillness, I noticed that the trees were losing their leaves. Slowly, one at a time they dropped down. The old was making room for the new that would come. The summer season of outer growth was ending, and now the fall season of transformation and inner growth was able to begin.

Sometimes we feel like those dried-up leaves—fragile, unimportant, unable to remain connected and fresh. That experience leaves us in a free-fall, drifting wherever our moods lead us or winds may blow us. Nothing can do this faster than a move to a foreign country where we are the "new kid on the block" in every respect. Our husbands are immediately welcomed into a new job with new friends. We on the other hand often have to fend for ourselves.

My husband and I with our two boys had moved to Italy a couple of days before Christmas. We had nowhere to go for

Christmas dinner, and all the restaurants were closed—things looked bleak. At this point I had a choice—to dwell in negative thoughts about our new duty station and ruin our family's Christmas, or give folks the benefit of the doubt—perhaps they just didn't know we were there. God reminded me that it was time again for some seasonal changes for our family.

In what season are you living? Are you resisting transformation, which could rid you of old, inflexible attitudes and replace them with God's views which are framed in mercy? Only as we are transformed and renewed can we discern His good, pleasing, and perfect will. As we lose our leaves in season, then God transforms us into His people who understand and know what He wants to do in us and through us—for His glory.

Romans 12:1–2 urges us to submit completely to God because of His mercy. Tell God that your life does belong to Him and that He can make the choices for you. Christ gave His life for us—we owe Him ourselves. We worship the Lord by giving Him our lives to mold and make them as He pleases.

Renewal begins with your heart and mind—on what you read, hear, and think. Reflect about how He wants you to live and study His Word for direction. As you follow these steps, you will know God's good, pleasing, and perfect will.

Ask

Am I holding and clinging to the old—locations, family, jobs, traditions, and so on—for security rather than trusting in Christ for the new?
Is it time for a new season in my life?
Will I resist or follow God's renewal?

Pray

Lord, You have always been faithful. Help me to trust You, follow You, and please You as this current season changes—and as new things replace old ones. Help me to welcome these transformations and these renewals, knowing that Your ways and Your plans are always good for us Your children and for our growth. In Jesus' Name, Amen.

by Eathel Weimer

GOD'S *Presence*

They got up and returned at once to Jerusalem. There they found the Eleven and those with them, assembled together and saying, "It is true! The Lord has risen and has appeared to Simon." Then the two told what had happened on the way, and how Jesus was recognized by them when He broke the bread.

LUKE 24:33–35 NIV

★ ★ ★

THE PHONE CALL I HAD BEEN WAITING FOR all morning finally came. To my delight my husband had already received written Permanent Change of Station (PCS) orders to the New England area. But in true Navy fashion things were about to change. He had called earlier that morning to tell me there was a chance that his orders might be changed. No changes—that was what I wanted to hear. I wanted orders that would allow us to live near my married son and his wife and visit back and forth like normal families! But the phone message confirmed my fears. We were moving again—to Italy.

We had lived in Italy seventeen years ago. Returning to live there as an older woman wasn't at the top of my "to do" list. Adjusting to another culture is easier when you are young, but the orders said to go, so preparations were in progress to do so. As I began to pack for the move, I became aware that God had something to teach me by wanting me to live in Italy again.

My husband was thrilled about the new orders as he would be part of a staff stationed on a ship deployed in the

Mediterranean Sea. Being on a ship and being able to minister to his shipmates was an ideal job for him. But Lord, what about me? This won't be ideal for me. He'll be gone quite a bit and I'll be in unfamiliar surroundings again all by myself.

Just as the disciples thought they were all alone on the road to Emmaus after the crucifixion, they discovered that Jesus had not abandoned them. He knew their disappointment that things just hadn't turned out as planned and joined them going the "wrong way." His presence dispelled their previous belief that He was dead (powerless). After being with Jesus and listening to Him, He didn't have to tell them to return to Jerusalem to share this "good news" with the other disciples. The fellowship they shared with Jesus along the "wrong way" going in the "wrong direction" compelled them to turn around and go back.

God reminded me that fellowship with Him is what is important whether it is in the USA or in another country. My orders are to fellowship with Him, then everything else falls into place. His presence is with us wherever we go. He knows our needs and fears and dispels them when we fellowship with Him. And the good news is that Jesus is alive and well and perfectly capable of meeting and equipping us for the ministry He is leading us to do. A change of orders can just be interpreted as a change in opportunity to share the good news in a new place.

Ask

What new opportunity is opening up with these unexpected new orders?
How can my home be an oasis for folks who are living in another country?

Pray

Lord, You know how much I resist change or challenges. Thank You that You always go before us just as the Shepherd always goes before His sheep, finding safe pastures. Help me to share this knowledge of Your nature with other spouses that struggle with change. In Jesus' Name, Amen.

by Vanessa Peters

"I WILL *Bless* YOU"

I am the God of your father Abraham. Do not be afraid, for I am with you; I will bless you and increase the number of your descendants for the sake of My servant Abraham.
GENESIS 26:24 NIV

★ ★ ★

I HAD JUST GOTTEN A CALL from one of my dearest friends, Christy. She'd arrived safely in the Azores at her husband's new assignment. With an ocean separating us, she felt a million miles away. I tried to sound cheerful. "How do you like it? I bet it's beautiful there!" "Actually," she replied in a sad voice, "it's been a really hard move. I miss all my friends so much. How am I ever going to replace you guys?"

With her words heavy on my heart, I opened to Genesis 26 and read the story of Isaac, a grown man who had just buried his father, the patriarch Abraham. In the midst of mourning his father's death, Isaac learns his usually fertile homeland is afflicted by a famine. Like most others of his time, he sets out for Egypt where he can find food and help for his family. While he was en route, God stopped him dead in his tracks: "Do not go down to Egypt; live in the land where I tell you to live. Stay in this land for a while, and I will be with you and will bless you" (Genesis 26:2–3 NIV).

Isaac didn't question God's sovereignty. He simply and promptly obeyed and planted his crops in that land, Gerar. "The same year he reaped a hundredfold, because the Lord blessed him" (Gen. 26:12 NIV). Here he was in the midst of a famine and by simply obeying—he could provide food for his family! As his prosperity continued, the inhabiting Philistines began to grow jealous, secretly stopping up his wells. Finally, King Abimelech ordered Isaac to move. Again, Isaac moved on without complaint or hesitation to the Valley of Gerar. There we see that God blessed Isaac with a plentiful water supply. But alas, the people there were jealous, too, quarreling over and stealing his wells. Each time, Isaac graciously moved to a new location, and each time God abundantly blessed his efforts. Isaac's physical location was irrelevant—his spiritual location was all that was needed to ensure his blessings.

God has a plan for us as believers and blesses us even in the most unlikely circumstances. When we're called to leave friends and family, comforts of a particular home, and the support of a loving church—He is right alongside us, just waiting to shower us with blessings! Like Isaac, we can expect to be blessed a hundredfold, even in the midst of a famine. And when we're asked to move *again*, we can model Isaac's obedience and move without complaint or worry, knowing that God keeps His promises to bless His children.

The next day, I sent Christy a birthday card. "Read Genesis 26," I wrote. "God has big plans for you in the Azores!"

Ask

Am I holding back from God in any area of my life because I fear the future?

If I'm called to move, will I go without complaint or worry?

Lord, I know my life is in Your hands. The military may think they determine our next assignment, but we know the when and where are really a result of Your hand working in our lives. Help us to trust You when friends and family are far away. Please bless us in the midst of famine and help us to give all the glory to You. In Jesus' Name, Amen.

by Lasana Ritchie

ABSORBING GOD'S *Goodness*

Be of sober spirit, be on the alert.
Your adversary, the devil, prowls around like
a roaring lion, seeking someone to devour.
1 PETER 5:8

★ ★ ★

"WHAT IF IT'S NOT A GOOD SCHOOL SYSTEM?" "What if we can't find a house that we can afford?" "What if we don't end up with good neighbors?" "What if I can't find a job?"

How often do our questions reveal the amount of fear in our hearts rather than the level of our faith? Moving in the military can require all the resources we can muster. The questions or fears can keep coming; thankfully, so does God's grace and goodness. What will we do with each?

Enjoy some lessons from a sponge. Sponges are not absorbent at only two times: when it is *already* saturated, and when it is *squeezed* tightly in your hand. In both instances a sponge is subject to the forces around it.

In the same way, when I'm so stressed with the future move that I am tense, irritable, and putting all my energy into my worries, I won't have much of anything left for soaking up the goodness of God or the provisions He has already given me. When I would rather bury my head in the sand, God asks me to trust Him. My stress squeezes me as I would squeeze a sponge. Even under the constant flow of God's grace and goodness, held taut, I couldn't soak up any more moisture than the little bit with which I might have started.

I could be a sponge fully saturated with the worries of my mind and the fears of my heart, and I would then be unable to absorb the blessings that God has sent my way to aid me in my transition. I would be saturated with all the wrong things. Dwelling on my problems with a worried heart is not living in an attitude of prayer, and faith can't grow with ground that's already saturated with worry.

How can I change to absorb God's goodness, grace, and provision for my move in the military? A good starting place is to begin spending time in God's presence, reading his Word, writing down the lessons I feel He is teaching me while I am listening to His Spirit within my heart. It will take time. Sponges can't absorb much when they are quickly whisked through the flow and go on their way. I must be still to absorb.

Ask

Am I squeezed by something I need to surrender to God?
Am I saturated with the wrong focus?
Do I need to spend more quality time in His presence, *allowing* Him to fill me?

Pray

Dear Lord, We can't will ourselves to be filled, and we can't fill ourselves. Please help us be willing to allow You to fill us. Teach us to be silent in Your presence and allow You full reign in our lives and hearts. Show us where fear is choking out faith, and restore to us Your peace in all our uncertainty. In Jesus' Name, Amen.

by Jocelyn Green

MAKING OURSELVES *Ready*

"Hallelujah! For the Lord our God, the Almighty, reigns. Let us rejoice and be glad and give the glory to Him, for the marriage of the Lamb has come and His bride has made herself ready." It was given to her to clothe herself in fine linen, bright and clean; for the fine linen is the righteous acts of the saints.
REVELATION 19:6–8

★ ★ ★

THERE WAS NO TIME TO LOSE. Ann Hardin's husband would be home from Iraq soon for environmental leave (R&R), and before he arrived, she had work to do! She lost weight, got in shape, and treated herself to her first pedicure. She stocked the kitchen with all his favorite foods and got her household in order just for the moment he walked in the door. She even planted flowers, which was no small feat in May in Anchorage, Alaska.

As Ann prepared herself and her household for her reunion with her husband, something else dawned on her. "Through all the things I wanted to get ready for my husband, my earthly bridegroom, the Lord showed me how much more I need to be getting ready for my heavenly bridegroom," she said. "The love and longing I have for my husband, I should have for my Lord."

God wants to be more to us than merely our Creator. By assuming the names of Bridegroom (*Nymphios*) and Husband (*Aner*), Jesus reveals the kind of intimate relationship He desires to have with us, His Bride. When He was born into this fallen world, He was leaving His Father's house to dwell among us. Christ offers Himself as our provider and protector, and has vowed his faithfulness and love to us not just "till death do us part," but forever.

In Matthew 25:1–13, Jesus tells the parable of ten virgins holding a night vigil for the bridegroom. When the five who ran out of oil for their lamps went to get more, the bridegroom came for those who were prepared. The story ends with, "Be on the alert then, for you do not know the day nor the hour" (Matthew 25:13).

Ann Spangler offers this "spiritual preparedness kit" so we can be like the wise virgins in the parable:

1. Repent daily (Matthew 3:2).
2. Get caught serving (Matthew 25:14–30).
3. Be quick to forgive (Matthew 18: 23–32).
4. Never let the sun go down on your anger (Ephesians 4:25–27).
5. Pray always (1 Thessalonians 5:17).
6. Give thanks in all circumstances (1 Thessalonians 5:18).
7. Be generous to the poor (Luke 12:33–34).
8. Remember, no matter what, that God is faithful (1 Corinthians 10:12–13).
9. Link your life with other believers (1 Corinthians 12:12–27).[2]

Hopefully, we will always be devoted to our husbands on this earth, whether they are present or absent from our homes. But just as Ann poured herself into preparing herself for her husband's homecoming, let us be faithful to prepare ourselves for our meeting with our heavenly bridegroom, as well.

Ask

Am I more concerned with my relationship with my earthly husband or my heavenly bridegroom?

What areas of my spiritual life need to be worked on before I can consider myself a prepared bride?

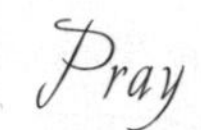

Lord, Help me begin to fathom the depths of Your love for me as my heavenly bridegroom and husband. May I daily seek to be worthy of such an honor by preparing my heart and mind with spiritual truths and disciplines. While my marriage is a gift from You, remind me that I can find true intimacy in my relationship with You. In Jesus' Name, Amen.

APPENDIX: KNOWING JESUS *Personally*

If you have not yet trusted Christ as your Savior, let today be the day that you invite Him to be Lord of your life. Without Christ, we have no hope in this life and no hope of being in heaven in the next. But because of Christ, we can accept eternal life as a free gift based on God's grace!

> "For the wages of sin is death, but the free gift of God is eternal life in Christ Jesus our Lord" (Romans 6:23).

Heaven is not something that we can earn or deserve on our own merits. We can't go to church enough, give enough money to charity, or be good enough in any way to pave our own way to heaven. But the good news is that we don't have to—because God's grace is offered to us as a gift!

> "For by grace you have been saved through faith; and that not of yourselves, it is the gift of God; not as a result of works, so that no one may boast" (Ephesians 2:8–9).

No one deserves to go to heaven, because we sin. Even the best of us do things that displease God.

> "For all have sinned and fall short of the glory of God" (Romans 3:23).
>
> "There is none who does good, there is not even one" (Romans 3:12).
>
> "For whoever keeps the whole law and yet stumbles in one point, he has become guilty of all" (James 2:10).

Because God is holy and just, this sin prevents us from being able to be in His presence.

> "The wages of sin is death" (Romans 6:23).

Because God also is not willing that any should perish, He sent His son, Jesus Christ, into the world as the perfect, blameless one to die for us. When He died, he paid the penalty for our sins and purchased a place in heaven for us.

> "But God demonstrates His own love toward us, in that while we were yet sinners, Christ died for us" (Romans 5:8).
>
> "For Christ also died for sins once for all, the just for the unjust, so that He might bring us to God" (1 Peter 3:18).
>
> "Jesus said to him, 'I am the way, and the truth, and the life; no one comes to the Father but through Me'" (John 14:6).

If you believe this much is true, you're on the right track. But you must go one step further and receive the gift of salvation by placing your personal faith in Christ, asking Him to be your Savior and Lord. Faith is turning from your sins and trusting in Jesus Christ alone for your eternal salvation.

> "But as many as received Him, to them He gave the right to become children of God, even to those who believe in His name" (John 1:12).
>
> "Whoever will call on the name of the Lord will be saved" (Romans 10:13).

Are you ready to invite Christ into your life? Pray to Him right now, acknowledging your sin and accepting the free gift of eternal life. Ask Him to show you how to live in a way that honors Him. The suggested prayer below may express the desire of your heart:

Dear Lord, Thank You for the gift of eternal life. I know I am a sinner and that I cannot save myself. I believe Jesus is the Son of God and that He died for my sins and rose again from the dead. I now put my complete trust in Him alone for eternal life. Thank You for saving me. Now, help me through Your Holy Spirit to live a life that honors You. In Jesus' Name, Amen.

If you prayed to receive Christ, rejoice! You just made the most important decision that you will ever make in your life. Find someone to share your news with, and seek out a Bible-teaching church where you can spend time with other

Christians and learn the Word of God. Make Bible reading and prayer a daily priority, and allow God to mold you into the person He wants you to be.

APPENDIX: RESOURCES FOR *Military Families*

WEB SITES

HopefortheHomeFront.com—Explores the emotional and spiritual battlegrounds common in the experience of today's military wife. *Hope for the Home Front* speaks from Marshéle Carter Waddell's personal experiences and offers Scriptural encouragement to millions of others who bear similar burdens of fear, loneliness, anger, disappointment, temptation, frequent moves, single parenting, and separation from loved ones.

Wivesoffaith.org—Wives of Faith is a faith-based military wives support organization that seeks to connect, encourage, and support military wives of all branches of service including active, Reserve, National Guard, and retired. Ladies who attend a WoF meeting discover a positive focus and an emphasis on hope. For more information on the annual national conference or to find or start a local chapter in your area, visit **www.wivesoffaith.org** or e-mail **sara@wivesoffaith.org** or **info@wivesoffaith.org**.

AGreaterFreedom.com—A faith-based military news site that reports the positive stories of what is happening in Iraq and the global war on terror as well as stories of what God is doing in the lives of service members and their families.

Military.com—The largest military and veteran membership organization that connects service members, military families, and veterans to all the benefits of service—government benefits, scholarships, discounts, lifelong friends, mentors, great stories of military life or missions, and much more. Online forums allow you to interact with other military wives dealing with deployment.

AmericaSupportsYou.mil—A great site that provides dozens of links to grassroots organizations that support our military and their families in a variety of ways.

SoldiersAngels.com—This is a fantastic organization that has multiple levels of organizations under it—everything from groups who make cookies for the troops to those who make quilts for the wounded.

Adopt-a-Chaplain.org—This is a great organization that supports our chaplains in the field who in turn support the troops.

ORGANIZATIONS

Family Life
www.familylife.com
1-800-FL-TODAY
Hop online or call them for the HomeBuilders Bible study for military couples.

Navigators Military Ministry
http://www.navigators.org/us/ministries/military
e-mail: milsupport@navigators.org
This ministry is composed of nearly four hundred workers serving Army, Navy, Air Force, Marine Corps, and Coast Guard personnel in the U.S. and overseas.

Campus Crusade Military Ministry
http://www.militaryministry.org/
1-800-444-6006
The Web site includes a variety of resources including PTSD healing (www.ptsdhealing.org), military marriage seminar schedules, and book, video, and music resources. Call or e-mail info@ptsdhealing.org to get in touch with counselors and prayer warriors. Check out www.excellentorpraiseworthy.com, their online devotional site.

Officers Christian Fellowship of the USA
www.ocfusa.org
1-800-424-1984
This fellowship is designed to build spiritual maturity in member military officers and to provide support, especially for transient officers. They offer the quarterly magazine *Command*.

Cadence International
www.cadence.org
1-800-396-6680
This nonprofit organization targets military singles, families, and youth through hospitality houses, retreats, Bible studies, and youth groups.

Christian Military Fellowship (CMF)
www.cmfhq.org
1-800-798-7875
CMF reaches out to all ranks, family members, and civilian employees. Members share their prayer requests with the home office, where they are published monthly and made available to the entire fellowship.

BOOKS

Adsit, Rev. Chris, Rev. Rahnella Adsit, and Marshéle Carter Waddell. *When War Comes Home: Christ-Centered Solutions for Wives of Combat Veterans*. Newport News, Va.: Military Press, Campus Crusade for Christ's Military Ministry, 2008.

Helps wives understand their husbands' post-traumatic stress and arms them with the biblical truth necessary to weather the storm of combat-related stress at home.

Dillow, Linda. *Calm My Anxious Heart*. Colorado Springs: NavPress, 1998.

A thoughtful, thorough treatment of worry and anxiety.

Ethridge, Shannon. *Every Woman's Battle*. Colorado Springs:

WaterBrook, 2003.

An excellent resource for every woman who struggles with sexual temptation or inappropriate emotional attachments.

Horn, Sara. *Weekend Warrior No More; Help and Hope for Reservists and Their Families During Deployment*. Dulles, Va.: Potomac Books, Inc., 2009.

A survival guide for reserve and guard spouses coping with the unfamiliar territory of deployment. This book offers hope, practical advice, and stories from those who have been there.

James, Carolyn Custis. *When Life and Beliefs Collide*. Grand Rapids: Zondervan, 2001.

How strong is your faith when life turns upside down? James addresses the importance of right theology in the face of tragedy.

Kay, Ellie. *Heroes at Home*. Bloomington, Minn.: Bethany House Publishers, 2002.

With a mixture of humor, stories, and practical tips, this uplifting book shows military families how to do things a little smarter.

Sedler, Michael. *Stop the Runaway Conversation*. Grand Rapids: Chosen Books, 2001.

A must read for anyone who has struggled with telling or listening to gossip (who hasn't?).

Vandesteeg, Carol. *When Duty Calls*. Enumclaw, Wash.: WinePress Publishing, 2001.

A comprehensive guide to equip military families for separations.

Waddell, Marshéle Carter. *Hope for the Home Front*. Birmingham, Ala.: New Hope Publishers, 2006. First published in 2003.

The author offers Scripture-based encouragement for the trials common to the military wife's unique lifestyle. An accompanying Bible study is also available.

Notes

Introduction

1. Charles A Wickman, compiler, *Praise! Our Songs and Hymns* (Grand Rapids: Singspiration Music, 1979), 378.

Section One: Taking Every Thought Captive

1. Jerry Bridges, *Trusting God: A Study Guide* (Colorado Springs: NavPress, 1989), 12.
2. John Ortberg, *The Life You've Always Wanted* (Grand Rapids: Zondervan, 1997), 102.
3. From *Streams of Living Water,* quoted in *A Place of Quiet Rest* by Nancy Leigh DeMoss (Chicago: Moody, 2000), 103.
4. Nancy Leigh DeMoss, *Lies Women Believe* (Chicago: Moody, 2001), 85.

Section Two: Guarding the Heart

1. Shannon Ethridge, *Every Woman's Battle* (Colorado Springs: WaterBrook Press, 2003), 94.
2. Josiah Bull, *But Now I See: The Life of John Newton* (Edinburgh, Scotland: Banner of Truth Trust, 1998), 358. First published in 1868.
3. C.S. Lewis, *The Weight of Glory* (New York: Macmillan, 1980), 4.
4. Michael Sedler, *Stop the Runaway Conversation* (Grand Rapids: Chosen Books, 2001), 36–42.

Section Three: Ambassadors for Christ

1. *Thorndike and Barnhart Advanced Dictionary*, Second edition (Glenview, Ill.: Scott Foresman and Company, 1974), s.v. "hospitality."

2. *Webster's New World College Dictionary*, Fourth edition (New York: MacMillan, 1999), s.v. "hospitable."

Section Four: Taking Orders

1. Linda Dillow, *Calm My Anxious Heart* (Colorado Springs: NavPress, 1998), 65.

2. Marvin Olasky, "Livingstone's Prayer," *World Magazine*, 6 Aug 05, accessed through http://www.worldmag.com/articles/10894.

Section Five: Total Surrender

1. Nancy Leigh DeMoss, *Surrender* (Chicago: Moody, 2003), 59.

2. Carolyn Custis James, *The Gospel of Ruth* (Grand Rapids: Zondervan, 2008), 84.

3. Grace Fox, *Moving from Fear to Freedom: A Woman's Guide to Peace in Every Situation* (Eugene, Ore.: Harvest House, 2007), 115–117.

4. John Ortberg, *The Life You've Always Wanted* (Grand Rapids: Zondervan, 1997), 82.

5. Joanna Weaver, *Having a Mary Heart in a Martha World: Finding Intimacy with God in the Busyness of Life* (Colorado Springs: WaterBrook, 2000), 55.

6. Edward W. Goodrick, John R. Kohlenberger III, and James A. Swanson, assoc. eds., *Zondervan NIV Exhaustive Concordance*, 2nd ed. (Grand Rapids: Zondervan, 1999), s.v. "Sovereign."

7. Jerry Bridges, *Trusting God: A Study Guide* (Colorado Springs: NavPress, 1989), 13.

8. Brennan Manning, *Ruthless Trust* (New York: HarperSanFrancisco, 2002), 96–97.

9. http://skdesigns.com/internet/articles/prose/niebuhr/serenity_prayer/

Section Six: The Price of Duty

1. Carolyn Custis James, *When Life and Beliefs Collide* (Grand Rapids: Zondervan, 2001), 73.
2. Marshéle Carter Waddell, *Hope for the Home Front* (Phoenix: One Hope Ministry, 2003), 64.

Section Seven: Active Duty Faith

1. Elisabeth Elliot, *Passion and Purity* (Tarrytown, N.Y.: Fleming H. Revell Company, 1984), 84.
2. Carolyn Custis James, *Lost Women of the Bible* (Grand Rapids: Zondervan, 2005), 180.
3. Strong's Concordance accessed through Blue Letter Bible (www.blueletterbible.com), s.v. *charis* (grace).
4. Marshéle Carter Waddell, *Hope for the Home Front* (Phoenix: One Hope Ministry, 2003), 29–30.
5. Elisabeth Elliot, *Passion and Purity*, 86.
6. http://songsandhymns.org/hymns/detail/abide-with-me-fast-falls-the-eventide, and http://songsandhymns.org/hymns/lyrics/abide-with-me-fast-falls-the-eventide.

Section Eight: Hope of Victory

1. Carolyn Custis James, *When Life and Beliefs Collide* (Grand Rapids: Zondervan, 2001), 71–72.
2. Ann Spangler, *Praying the Names of Jesus* (Grand Rapids: Zondervan, 2006), 264.

MEET THE *Contributors*

Pamela Anderson, U.S. Marine Corps

Pamela Anderson lives and writes in Jacksonville, North Carolina. She and her husband, Chaplain John Anderson, have served in three different military duty stations, beginning in 2002. Her daughter Tiffany is nine years old and is her favorite walking buddy. Pamela's undergraduate degree is in sacred music from North Central Bible College. She enjoys playing the piano or singing with any praise team or church choir who will have her. Her other interests include reading and enjoying the mountains and coasts of North Carolina.

Sarah Ball, U.S. Army

Growing up as a missionary kid on Guam, Sarah Ball decided she didn't want to marry a pastor or a military man. Today she is married to both—a pastor and a soldier—in her husband Doug, an active duty Army chaplain. They've now been married eleven years and have four children.

After obtaining her B.S. in education from John Brown University, Sarah married Doug and spent three years teaching middle school English. Once their first child was born, she changed her focus to home and ministry. Sarah and Doug lived in Nebraska for five years, where Doug pastored a church and served with the Nebraska National Guard. Their second child was born while Doug was deployed to Bosnia, and the third while he was deployed to Iraq. Their children are Rachel, age 8, Robbie, age 5, Laura, age 2, and Levi, born in January 2008. Sarah enjoys working in ministries like AWANA, MOPS, and Protestant Women of the Chapel (PWOC), and doing some freelance writing as time allows.

Rebekah Benimoff, U.S. Army

Rebekah Benimoff grew up in Austin, Texas. She and her husband, Roger, met at Texas State University, where she earned a B.S. in education, with a specialization in early childhood education. Roger and Rebekah have two very active and creative little boys: Tyler, age 9, and Blaine, age 6. Roger is an Army chaplain who has seventeen years of military service: nine with the National Guard, and eight serving on active duty.

Currently Rebekah has been sharing her experiences, memories, writings, and personal journal entries for an autobiographical book slated to be published by Crown in the spring of 2009. *Faith Under Fire* focuses on how Roger's time in Iraq challenged his faith and their marriage as he struggled with PTSD and compassion fatigue upon his return home.

Rebekah has enjoyed serving in PWOC, leading prayer groups, and working with praise teams as she and Roger have moved from post to post. Rebekah enjoys reading, writing, singing, hiking, and exploring local attractions with her family. The Benimoff family is currently stationed in San Antonio, Texas.

Paulette Harris, U.S. Air Force

Paulette Harris is a freelance author/speaker in Colorado. She and her husband have a heart to help the body of Christ understand and accept disabled people. Her husband is retired Air Force, and they have been married for thirty-nine years. She taught elementary children and youth groups, and worked in social services for years before retiring. She enjoys her two children and five grandchildren. Her hobbies include reading and reviewing books, golfing, gardening, writing, and animals. She has started work on her fifth novel. For more about Paulette, visit: www.pauletteharris.biz and www.comeandsitawhile.blogspot.blog.com.

Jill Hart, U.S. Air Force

Jill Hart is the founder of Christian Work at Home Moms, CWAHM.com. Jill is a contributing author in *The Business Mom Guide Book, I'll Be Home For Christmas,* and *Laundry Tales—To Lighten Your Load*. She has articles published across the Web on sites like DrLaura.com and ClubMom.com. Jill and her husband, Allen, who served in the U.S. Air Force for five years, reside in Nebraska with their two children. During his military career, Allen and Jill served as leaders in the Protestant Youth of the Chapel (PYOC) program and worked closely with the Navigator and Cadence ministries on base. Allen now works as a computer contractor on the base where he served, and they enjoy being a part of the military community they live in and serving those who are serving our country.

Sara Horn, U.S. Navy Reserves

Sara Horn is an award-winning writer who twice traveled to the Middle East to document stories of Christians serving in the midst of the Iraq War for her first book, 2005 Gold Medallion nominee *A Greater Freedom: Stories of Faith from Operation Iraqi Freedom* that she wrote with bestselling author Oliver North. She is also the author of *Help and Hope for Reservists and Their Families During Deployment,* due to be released in spring 2009. Her husband, a Navy reservist for more than eleven years, was deployed in 2007 to Iraq. They have one son.

Sara started Wives of Faith (www.wivesoffaith.org), a national military wives support organization, at the end of 2006. She maintains a blog frequented by military wives at www.sarahorn.com and serves as an occasional columnist for Military.com. A graduate of Union University, Sara stays busy with writing projects and with her work in Wives of Faith. She enjoys speaking to groups and is passionate about encouraging and supporting military wives of all branches of service. E-mail her at sara@sarahorn.com.

Denise McColl, U.S. Navy

A native of Washington, D.C., Denise McColl earned a degree from George Mason University. She married her husband, Angus, three days after he received his commission as a Naval officer, and they raised five daughters. Denise mentored many women and is the author of *Footsteps of the Faithful: Victorious Living and the Military Life* (Campus Crusade for Christ, 1994). Shortly after Angus retired from the Navy, he and Denise celebrated their twenty-fifth wedding anniversary in May 2007. Six weeks later, she was diagnosed with the brain cancer that took her life on March 29, 2008.

Lori Mumford, U.S. Coast Guard

Lori Mumford currently lives in Juneau, Alaska, with her husband and their three children. She keeps busy most of the year homeschooling all three. She enjoys Nordic skiing in the winter and running in the summer if not catching that rare day of sunshine for beach play. She's a graduate of Indiana University in medical technology with an M.S. in anthropology from the University of Oregon. Her husband is a chief petty officer, and they've lived the Coast Guard life for seventeen years. As he approaches retirement, they continue to trust God in teaching them what is best for them and directing them in the way they should go (Isaiah 48:17–18).

Vanessa Peters, U.S. Air Force

Vanessa Peters spent seven years as an Air Force spouse and is adjusting to civilian life with her family, which includes three children, aged 6, 4, and 3. Currently, they reside in Michigan where her husband is training to be a missionary pilot/mechanic. Vanessa received her B.A. degree in American studies and Christian studies at Hillsdale College. She now serves as a homemaker and also enjoys Bible study, books, music, scrapbooking, traveling, and jogging. She is a contributor to www.excellentorpraiseworthy.com, the online devotional of

Campus Crusade's Military Ministry.

Lasana Ritchie, U.S. Navy

Lasana Ritchie has a B.S. in art education, an A.B. in English education from Indiana Wesleyan University, and a double masters in both from St Francis University. She has taught every grade from kindergarten through college, but prefers art in elementary school. She is currently working on a novel, but spends most of her time raising four fantastic children and making pottery on the potter's wheel for craft fairs, friends, and family. Her husband, Gordon, is in his eighteenth year of serving the Navy. She would like little more than to have a log cabin in the woods, down the wooded path from a studio, and travel the world to view art and sample coffee! Her biggest challenge is to live in the present moment.

Sheryl Shearer, U.S. Navy

Sheryl Shearer, author and perpetual student, is the spouse of an active-duty Naval chaplain. She is mother and home educator to their four daughters. Additionally, Sheryl holds a Bachelor of Music degree from Minnesota State University at Moorhead, a Master of Arts in Theological Studies from the Assemblies of God Theological Seminary in Springfield, Missouri, where she is currently a candidate for the Master of Divinity degree.

Ten moves (thus far) under her belt—within fourteen years of marriage to husband, Brian—qualify Sheryl as an expert relocator. Eight of those years have been spent in active duty service: three in the Army and five with the Navy / Marine Corps. In the Shearers' current home city of Chicago, Illinois, Sheryl serves as an adult educator, leading adult Bible studies in her local church. In her spare moments, Sheryl enjoys reading, blogging, playing the piano, running, traveling, and attempting to solve the *Chicago Tribune*'s daily crossword puzzle.

Ronda Sturgill, U.S. Air Force

Author and retreat/seminar speaker, Ronda Sturgill is the wife of an active duty U.S. Air Force chaplain. A paraplegic as the result of a horseback riding accident in 1972, Ronda is a former world-class archer on the United States Wheelchair Athletic Team. As a Christian communicator, Ronda motivates and inspires people to find hope by applying biblical principles to their lives. Ronda ministers to both military and civilian audiences.

Ronda is a graduate of the University of Maryland. She has written three Bible studies. *Wives of the Warriors: Living Confidently in Christ* has encouraged women all over the world in their faith walk and is available from most online bookstores. *Desperate Housecries: Discovering a Genuine Hope in God* and *Extreme Makeover: Heart Edition* are available for a free download from the Protestant Women of the Chapel Web site, www.pwoconline.org. Other publications include personal stories in the *God Allows U-Turns* series, as well as several magazine articles.

Ronda and her husband, Tim, have one grown son. For more information about Ronda, visit her Web site at www.finding-hopeinhim.com.

Marshéle Carter Waddell, U.S. Navy

Marshéle Carter Waddell served with her husband, CDR (ret) Mark Waddell, a career U.S. Navy SEAL, for twenty-three years around the world. Her first two books, *Hope for the Home Front: Winning the Emotional and Spiritual Battles of a Military Wife* and its companion Bible study, *Hope for the Home Front Bible Study*, arm other military wives with God's promises of His presence, power, and protection. She is also coauthor of *When War Comes Home: Christ-Centered Solutions for Wives of Combat Veterans*. Together with their three children, the Waddells have endured many lengthy separations and frequent deployments for combat duty, special operations training, and real-world conflicts for two decades.

Marshéle has published articles in *Today's Christian Woman, Marriage Partnership, Virtue, Command,* and *Military Lifestyle* magazines and is a contributor to CBN's Web site, www.cbn.com. She is an international speaker for military ministry and women's events, most recently at Times Square Church in New York City. She is the founder of One Hope Ministry, based in Monument, Colorado, where she resides with her husband and three children.

Eathel Weimer, U.S. Navy

Eathel Weimer graduated from the University of Georgia with a degree in speech pathology. She has also worked as a church preschool teacher, an InterVarsity Christian Fellowship staff worker with college students, and most recently as a departmental secretary with the U.S. Navy and at the Coast Guard Academy, officially retiring in 1999.

Eathel's husband was a Navy chaplain for thirty years, and they had the privilege of ministering together to sailors, Marines, and Coast Guard members all over the world. During this time Eathel also enjoyed entertaining in their home, leading Bible studies for women and working with MOPS (Mothers of Preschoolers). Their children (two married sons) and grandchildren fill their time now as well as the activities of the chapel Bill is serving in Florida.

ABOUT THE *Author*

Jocelyn Green is an award-winning freelance writer and editor and an active member of the Evangelical Press Association. She graduated from Taylor University in Upland, Indiana, in 1999 *magna cum laude* with a B.A. in English, concentration in writing. After working for a year in Taylor's university relations department, she moved to Washington, D.C., and served as the editor and project manager for the Council for Christian Colleges & Universities (CCCU). She and her husband, Rob, a Coast Guard officer, married July 5, 2003, at the Ft. Myer Army Base chapel at Arlington National Cemetery, and immediately transferred to Rob's next station in Homer, Alaska.

Rob has been a member of the Coast Guard for fifteen years—first as a volunteer Auxiliarist, then as a Coast Guard Academy cadet, a commissioned officer, and now an Auxiliarist. In 2004, after ten years of Active Duty service, Rob and Jocelyn moved to Cedar Falls, Iowa, where Rob owns and manages CutterAgent.com, a graphic design and production company servicing the needs of Coast Guard units worldwide.

Jocelyn has been freelance writing full-time since then, working with clients such as the CCCU, Taylor University, Eastern University, Indiana Wesleyan University, General Mills, Nestle, and Publix. She has had dozens of articles published in the following magazines: *Christianity Today, Campus Life's Ignite Your Faith, Today's Christian, ZIA Magazine, Today's Pentecostal Evangel, InSite,* and *EFCA Today.* Most of the articles can be read at www.jocelyngreen.com. Email her at jocelyn@jocelyngreen.com.

Jocelyn and Rob have two children.